THE TASTE OF OUR TIME

Collection planned and directed by

ALBERT SKIRA

PARIS IN THE PAST

FROM FOUQUET TO DAUMIER
One volume

PARIS IN OUR TIME

FROM IMPRESSIONISM TO THE PRESENT DAY
One volume

★

TEXT BY PIERRE COURTHION

Translated by Stuart Gilbert

Paris in Our Time

SKIRA

Famous Places as seen by Great Painters

Paris is a city where nature has never worn out her welcome, but continues to thrive even in the ultra-modern quarters. The Seine with its shady banks and sunny quays provides a perfect haven of flowers and greenery, while the whole city is dotted with parks and gardens. The Impressionists and after them the Fauves roamed Paris with eager, understanding eyes, recording the tremor of the trees along the avenues, the shimmering surface of the river, old walls glowing in the sun, chimney smoke gathering into wisps of cloud above the rooftops. On monuments mellowed by time the faintest shades of color flicker as if seen across a tenuous veil. This unique light of Paris, made of sunshine and mist, gives every element its rightful place and tone in the panorama. Even the Eiffel Tower, modern times' great contribution to the silhouette of Paris, blends with the monuments of the past, a soaring, bodiless piece of architecture giving the full measure of the sky above the city. The best painters of the present day no longer linger over anecdote and detail; their broad synthetic vision embraces the seen and unseen treasures of a city as rich in past glories as it is rich in promise for the future.

JONGKIND - MONET - RENOIR - DEGAS - MANET - MORISOT
SEURAT - SIGNAC - DUBOIS-PILLET - HAYET - VAN GOGH
PISSARRO - LAUTREC - BONNARD - VUILLARD - MATISSE
MARQUET - BRAQUE - ROUAULT - UTRILLO - ROUSSEAU - GLEIZES
LAURENCIN - LÉGER - DELAUNAY - BAZAINE - GROMAIRE
CHAGALL - PICASSO - DE STAËL - VIEIRA DA SILVA - BEAUDIN

FROM REALISM TO IMPRESSIONISM

NOTHING is more striking in the history of art—and indeed the history of culture in general—than the sudden breaks of continuity which take place when after a slow, sedate advance "from precedent to precedent" a more adventurous generation comes to the fore, eager for new worlds to conquer. In the case of art these bloodless revolutions are often the work of a quite small group of rebels or even a single man in whom the smoldering unrest of several generations bursts into flame.

At first sight, for contemporaries, it seems as if the entire past has been done away with, ruthlessly and irrevocably: the artists' feeling for plastic values, their way of seeing, their sense of color. Then gradually, once the initial shock has worn off, the new discoveries fall into place, time irons out asperities, and what once looked startling comes to seem normal and familiar.

Painting with a set subject, a heritage of the Renaissance, had long held the field; even Delacroix when he invented a "psychology of color" thought best to keep to it. But once the romantics and realists had turned their back on an art whose painterly aspirations were so often cramped by the need for story-telling, every vanguard artist sought primarily to achieve a personal method of expression in which he could exploit the properties of his medium to the utmost.

Hence the change-over from Realism to Impressionism; the end of academic "finish" and the curriculum of the art-schools. The new men sought not merely to retain the freshness of the sketch but made it their chief objective; rapid execution, *peinture claire* and an alert sensibility were the order of the day.

"You are a shining exception in the decrepitude that has come upon your art," Baudelaire wrote to Manet on May 11, 1865, à propos of *Olympia* which had just been exhibited and had come in for a violently hostile reception. What did our great French poet, ardent champion though he was of the "new painting," mean by the reference to decrepitude? He had in mind the decline of atelier training—that is to say of groups of young men studying art together under a common master—and the end of the age-old tradition of the apprentice craftsman.

It is certain that the teaching of the plastic arts was then at a low ebb and the masters at the Ecole des Beaux-Arts (many of whom did not even really understand the classical art they made so much of) usually bestowed their favors on pupils devoid of personality who kept discreetly to the beaten track.

Forward-looking painters were now "lone wolves," resentful of discipline and no longer willing to pander to the sentimental tastes of the public of the day. Each claimed an absolute liberty to follow his own bent, the result being "a division of labor" and "a dispersal of endeavor" [1]. Ever more isolated, the artist felt free to invent his own language and under the influence of Corot to paint in bright, luminous colors, at a far remove from Courbet's sedulously lowered tones, Daumier's chiaroscuro and the shadowy forest interiors of Barbizon.

Thus it was that after the somber *Footbridge to the Ile Saint-Louis* (1854) and *Pont Notre-Dame* (1862) now in the Louvre, Jongkind, greatly daring, bathed his *Notre-Dame from the Quays* in richly glowing light. In it we have a view of Paris seen from the Quai de La Tournelle on the Left Bank, with the archbishop's gardens to the tip of which, facing prow-wise up the Seine, the Morgue had been recently transferred.

This remarkable picture heralded the dawn of modernism, the new art that was to triumph in the second half of the 19th century. At the time Jongkind, "a blond giant with Delft-blue eyes" [2], had found a guardian angel in the person of Madame Fesser, a mustached matron, wife of a pastry-cook, who kept a stern check on his propensities for drinking and womanizing.

Johann-Barthold Jongkind (1819-1891). Notre-Dame from the Quays, 1864. Mme Cachin-Signac Collection, Paris.

He was living in Montparnasse, not far from his strong-minded benefactress who insisted on accompanying him whenever he went out and choosing his friends for him. Among the favored few was Boudin, and she also extended her patronage to Claude Monet, a young man who had just finished his military service in the African light cavalry.

Monet was twenty-six when he painted his *Quai du Louvre*, with the Pont-Neuf on the left and in the center, rising above the leafage of the Vert-Galant, the Pantheon dome. With its pale blue sky and shimmering air dappled with fleecy clouds, the picture is a delightful symphony of light.

During the year when Monet painted this gay, sunlit quay, dotted with pedestrians, cabs and victorias (the scene might be sub-titled "the heyday of the parasol"), Renoir was sharing Bazille's Paris apartment in the Rue Visconti. On Fridays Manet and Nadar often called on Baudelaire, then under treatment in Dr Duval's "water cure" clinic in the Rue du Dôme. Shortly

Claude Monet (1840-1926). Quai du Louvre (fragment), 1866.
Municipal Museum, The Hague.

before the poet's death (1867), the Goncourt brothers championed the cause of the new art in a novel written in collaboration.
One of the characters in *Manette Salomon* is a painter who has
all the marks of an Impressionist. "In summer, in autumn, at all
hours, morning, noon and sunset, Crescent recorded the emo-
tions quickened by the scene before him, and he had a wonderful
gift for rendering the sensations of each moment... Starting
out from memories and sketches, he transferred on to his
canvases the ever-changing aura of the passing hours that
wove itself around the rigid sameness of the motif, tree or
landscape—in a word, their atmosphere" [3].

Auguste Renoir (1841-1919). The Pont des Arts and the Institute, 1868.
Mrs Richard N. Ryan Collection, New York.

Who was the first painter to record these transient effects, nuances of light and sensibility, subtle as Debussy's music? The question is hard to answer. Courbet may be said to have anticipated the practices of the open-air painters in his *Girls on the Banks of the Seine*, yet this picture lacks the boldness of their approach to nature. Perhaps the palm should go to Manet and the *Concert in the Tuileries Gardens*, in which he carefully distributed his friends—Baudelaire, Gautier, Offenbach, Fantin-Latour—among the crowd, seated on chairs or leaning against trees. All Manet is already in this picture; the plangent tones of black he took from Goya, the billowing pink of skirts, a perfect consonance of figures and landscape.

Five years after painting this Parisian afternoon piece which, when exhibited in Martinet's gallery on the Boulevard des Italiens, created something of a scandal owing to the novelty of the subject, Manet started work on his big, panoramic view of the 1867 World's Fair.

The inauguration took place in spring and all summer the Parisians lived in an atmosphere of *fêtes vénitiennes*, fireworks and hectic gaiety. Headwaiters were at their most obsequious, buses packed with sightseers, cabdrivers always threatening to strike for higher fares and an incredible number of buildings of all shapes and styles had sprung up like mushrooms on the Champ-de-Mars, in a green profusion of trees and arbors.

A Parisian, son of well-to-do Parisian parents, and a revolutionary in spite of himself, Manet was the typical man-about-town of the mid-19th century. Carrying a light cane, wearing a fawn overcoat and top hat, a smile forever on his lips, he was often to be seen taking his constitutional from the fashionable Tortoni café to the Guerbois before returning to his home in the Batignolles district.

When visiting the Guerbois café, among whose habitués were Zola, Desboutins, Fantin-Latour and Degas, "Manet made a point of wearing showy trousers, a short coat, a flat-brimmed hat tilted well on the back of his head, and elegant suede gloves. He had no use for Bohemianism, sartorial or temperamental, and was by way of being a dandy. Fair, with a small, thin beard trimmed to two neat points, he might have passed for nothing more than this, were it not for the remarkable vivacity of his eyes, small pale-grey eyes well assorted with the slightly ironic curve of his thin lips. There was much of the Parisian gamin in his make-up and, though the most kind-hearted of men, he was apt to indulge in sarcastic, often cutting sallies" [4].

It was as the result of one of these that he fell foul of his friend Edmond Duranty, one of the pillars of the Guerbois group, and promptly fought a duel with him—only to make it up again at the café the same evening. After editing a short-lived review called *Le Réalisme*, Duranty—whom some believed to be a natural son of Prosper Mérimée—set to work on a book entitled *La Nouvelle Peinture*. "He had a mild, melancholy face with features of a singular delicacy and always spoke rather slowly, in low tones, with a slight, vaguely English accent. He lived in a ground-floor room near the Guerbois, and his chief interests in life were his pets: a cat, a dog, a magpie. Duranty was fair, very bald and had gentle but shrewdly observant blue eyes" [4].

Later, round about 1878, the Guerbois group migrated to the Nouvelle Athènes café, where Manet, his arrival heralded by the grating of the glass door of the café upon the sanded floor, always went straight to his wonted seat next to that of Degas. In *Confessions of a Young Man* George Moore gives a description of Degas' appearance at the time. "He is a round-shouldered man in a suit of pepper and salt. There is nothing very trenchantly French about him, except his large necktie" [5]. With these two masters of an older generation the Impressionists-to-be rubbed shoulders, as did the Anglo-Irish writer, now so devoted to Paris that he came there every winter.

ATMOSPHERE:
SMOKE AND MIST IN SUNLIGHT

A<small>LMOST</small> overnight, though actually the city had not changed in the least, Paris had acquired for the artist who could see it with understanding eyes a "new look": a color, an aspect and an atmosphere in which the most fugitive light effects, the merest ripple of the leaves of the trees along the Seine, a brief shimmer of the sun-steeped air possessed, if only for a magic moment, a value that transcended time, an intimation of eternity.

Thus it was that, even before Monet's famous sunrise scene *Impression: soleil levant* (from which Impressionism derived its name), some of the new painters sought to capture this atmosphere of Paris in the seventies, notably in renderings of such typical Seine-side streets as the Quai Malaquais, where we seem to get a snatch of the very perfume of the city.

The historical background meant next to nothing to them. Renoir, for example, when he painted the Quai Malaquais, was probably unaware of the fact that, before the quay was built, this part of the Seine bank was called Le Marais de la Grenouillère (the "froggery"), though the name should have appealed to him, since he had so much enjoyed painting (in Monet's company) the other "Grenouillère", a popular bathing-place at Bougival, near Paris. All that counted was the here-and-now: sunlit foliage, the ribbons on a girl's hat fluttering in a light breeze. Renoir's way, as Geffroy. speaking of his landscapes, observed twenty-four years later, "was to record these scenes hastily, just as they flashed upon the eye, lit up by vagrant sunbeams" [6].

In 1872, with rapid brushstrokes, at once firm and fluent, evoking the season, the hour of day and the weather, the exact look of earth and sky at a precise and pregnant moment,

Claude Monet (1840-1926). The Pont-Neuf, ca. 1872.
Emery Reves Collection, New York.

Monet painted the Pont-Neuf. Here there is nothing to remind
us of the cheerful crowds, the gaiety and laughter of high
summer. Rain is coming down in torrents, and hurrying along
under umbrellas, the passers-by cast wavering shadows on
the darkly glistening sidewalk. It is not too much to say that
no artist has ever evoked to better effect the nostalgic charm

of a wet day in Paris, when the atmosphere has the faintly iridescent, grey-green sheen of an aquarium. Some warmth still lingers in the air and its moisture, though insidious, is not displeasing. A tug-boat has just gone by and, as it whistles, launches a playful puff of steam towards the statue of Henry IV on the far bank.

The Impressionists were the first, after Corot, to make bold to tackle scenes of nature in which there is nothing—by which I mean nothing in the way of solid objects—and consisting solely of empty spaces traversed by the fleeting modulations of air and water.

Held by the glamour of the ephemeral, they sank their vision in a haze of broken gleams, the mirage of a "rainbow palette." In these scintillating works, interrogatory rather than affirmative, the fixity of classical art gives place to ceaseless movement. Paris as seen through the eyes of the Impressionists is a place where it is often raining or snowing, a city bathed in misty air and subject to the abrupt variations of temperature, colors and light on which they ring the changes so effectively, catching their most transient effects, the sudden glory of a flower in a girl's hat, the strident yellow of a bus, the greenish glint of water mirroring the brightly colored hulls of boats.

The artist who has rendered best this atmosphere of misty deliquescence was Claude Monet, notably in the series of pictures painted at Saint-Lazare station, for example the *Pont de l'Europe* in which he brings out to perfection the effect (rather like that of Loie Fuller's skirt dances, all the rage at Paris in the early nineties) of this ballet of interweaving lights and shades and glancing vapors, telling out against the gaunt anatomy of the great railway bridge.

Better than any other, Monet with his light, tremulous veils of color reveals the most fortuitous and fleeting aspects of the everyday world, in all their infinitely subtle modulations.

"It is precisely these sudden gleams, the magical light that plays on the surfaces of things," he wrote to his dealer Durand-Ruel, "that I am trying to capture—light that has the dove's-breast hues of shot silk or the blue glints of flaming punch."

And it was Monet who in these early years of Impressionism showed most fondness for the Parisian scene—unlike his friends who seemed at this time to prefer the countryside and stretches

Claude Monet (1840-1926). Saint-Lazare Station, 1877.
Mr and Mrs Minot K. Millikin Collection, New York.

Claude Monet (1840-1926). Saint-Lazare Station: the Pont de l'Europe, 1877.
Musée Marmottan, Paris.

of the river bathed in the mellow light of the Ile-de-France.
Though he painted the Canal Saint-Martin, Sisley rarely looked
to Paris for his motifs and it was only later that Pissarro produced his many evocations of the boulevards. As for Renoir,
mere bricks and mortar had little interest for him; what held

his gaze was a pretty woman passing in the street or an alluring incident of everyday life—all that might spell the pleasure of youth's observant gaze.

Cézanne made very few pictures of Paris, a city in which he never really felt at ease. However, in 1872 he painted the Halle aux Vins as seen from the window of his apartment in the Rue de Jussieu and, later, the *Quai de Bercy* (Kunsthalle, Hamburg) with a blue sky shot with pearly luster and "a huge shapeless mass of clouds looming up on the horizon" (Fénéon).[7] In that picture the solidity of the brushwork and close-knit composition showed how little the Aix master was in sympathy with the methods of the Impressionists. True, he had been persuaded to join forces with them in the early combative days, but he had never subscribed whole-heartedly to their theories of art and, like Degas and Renoir, ended up by severing his connection with the movement.

What the Impressionists show us is life's most transient aspects, a world without stability, a Paris neither durable nor solid, but "such stuff as dreams are made of," evanescent as morning dew or flowers that live for a day. In this new art all is clouds and smoke, the sparkle of ruffled water, and when night falls and gas lamps begin to twinkle in the smoke-dimmed air, even the passers-by seem wraith-like, figments of a dream.

PARIS AT PLAY

B<small>UT</small> this escape from life was not confined to contemplation of drifting clouds and glancing streams. It also found an outlet in the theater, in entertainments that give the rhythms of normal existence a quicker tempo, the brief thrill of a crowded hour.

One of the results, it seems, of the military disaster of 1870 was a vast enthusiasm for the theater, and meanwhile the magnificent Paris Opera House, work on which had been begun in 1861 under the direction of Charles Garnier, was nearing completion.

To this period dates the "ballet pantomime" *Coppelia*, and now for the first time the effects of gas footlights found their way into painting, Degas being the pioneer in this new field. After a cautious beginning with meticulously accurate depictions (largely based on photographs), he moved on to a broader execution, interspersed with large tracts of flat color, and finally to the bold, forthright design of his pastels in which he makes the most of the rich, powdery quality of the medium. Nothing, indeed, could be more enchanting than his scenes of dancers poised lightly near the footlights, while behind them, like a Greek chorus, the group of *petits sujets* perform their "variations."

It must not be forgotten that as far back as 1862, when a company of Spanish dancers was appearing at the Paris Hippodrome, Manet had painted his *Spanish Ballet*, which he followed up with two other canvases: *Masked Ball at the Opera* and *Bar at the Folies-Bergère*. But it was left to Degas to celebrate the contemporary stage under its essentially Parisian aspects, and little of an Impressionist as he may seem in other respects, the broadly orchestrated movements and gestures of the ballerinas flitting across the stage in Degas' canvases are in the spirit of Impressionism.

He spent much time working in the old opera house in the Rue Le Peletier and his friend Désiré Dihau, bassoonist in the orchestra, with whom he often dined at Mère Lefebvre's restaurant in the Rue de la Tour-d'Auvergne, saw to it that he was given a convenient place to sketch from. It was while the Opera was in the Rue Le Peletier that the management had the idea of admitting regular patrons to the dancers' foyer; and it was in this opera house that the first performances of *Tannhäuser*, *Faust* and *Robert le Diable* were staged. In Degas' two pictures of the ballet of the last-named opera, he brings out to wonderful effect the contrast between the dimly lit auditorium—the real world—and the fictive world, bathed in light, where the dancers are evolving in the improbable setting of a convent. The more striking of these two pictures is the tall canvas now in the Metropolitan Museum, in which we see Hecht, one of Manet's dilettante friends, looking through his opera glasses, and in profile, facing the opposite direction, Dihau with his bassoon.

Next came the *Ecole de Danse* in which figures for the first time the spiral staircase that was so long one of the "properties" of Degas' studio. Here we have variations on the play of light coming from different directions, and in the lay-out unexpected breaks, in the Japanese manner—then a novelty in French art. Thus the figures of the dancers coming down the steps are cut short half way up the legs by the frame, the floor is represented as if seen from above, and on the faded plush of the bench in the foreground lie some discarded dancing sandals. A dancer is seated in half-shadow and behind her other girls are weaving, light as flowers, the patterns of a dance, while in a brightly lit backroom some of the younger pupils are practising toe-dancing.

At this time Degas was living in the Rue Blanche, looked after by Clotilde, a maid "like the soubrette in a French comedy." "If you like metaphors, however far-fetched," he wrote to

Edgar Degas (1834-1917). Ecole de Danse, 1873.
Corcoran Gallery of Art, Washington, D. C.

Fröhlich, "I might say that to produce good fruit one should be like a tree trained on an espalier; your arms stretched out, you stay put all your life, your mouth open to gobble up whatever comes your way."

Degas also gives us glimpses of Paris streets and shops in his scenes of milliners and women ironing. Decidedly unflattering were the poses he sometimes inflicted on his models

Edgar Degas (1834-1917). The Ballet of Robert le Diable, 1872.
By Courtesy of the Metropolitan Museum of Art, New York.

Edouard Manet (1832-1883). At the Café, 1878.
Oskar Reinhart Collection, Winterthur.

in this phase, making them squat ungainly in the bathtub, "bulging like over-ripe pumpkins"[7]. But he soon reverted to his dancers and music-hall singers, often doing them in pastel, a medium to which he gave an aerial freshness all his own.

Auguste Renoir (1841-1919). At the Milliner's, ca. 1876. By Courtesy ▶ of the Fogg Art Museum, Harvard University, Cambridge, Mass.

Until he lost his sight, the ballet dancer was his never-failing source of inspiration; on the stage or leaning against a pillar in the foyer, bowing to take a call, or resting in her dressing-room, hands on her hips, right leg stretched forward.

From Naples on January 17, 1886, Degas, still in the prime of life, wrote to a sculptor friend: "I have a feeling that every-thing in me is getting atrophied, the heart excepted. And even the heart has something artificial about it. My little dancers have sewn it up in a purse of pink satin, slightly faded like their dancing sandals" [8]. But Degas was neurasthenic; actually his hand had lost nothing of its cunning and Renoir, seven years younger, looking at his charcoal drawings, exclaimed that they might be "a bit of the Parthenon." Degas' comment on Renoir, who viewed the Parisian scene from a different angle, was that "he sprinkles his canvases with butterflies."

Renoir saw Paris through a lover's eyes. *At the Milliner's* shows us a charming customer in the throes of choosing a new hat. As in *The Box at the Theater* all is throbbing color, warm tones shot with coppery gleams—sensuous appeal. And the young woman, with her auburn hair, her elegant profile, and the gay red ribbon knotted round her neck, has that "Parisian air" we find again in the portrait of Jeanne Samary which now hangs in the Green Room of the Comédie Française.

We see the Parisienne under two aspects in the little dress-maker's assistant of the *Moulin de la Galette* and the young woman of *Dancing in Town*, in which the graceful profile of Madame Renoir tells out against Lhote's black coat (Lhote was one of the painter's friends) with the greenery of a hothouse in the background.

Mention may here be made of some of the cafés which were now our painters' meeting-places. The Guerbois and Nouvelle Athènes had been succeeded by Reichshoffen's tavern and the brasserie-concert on the Boulevard Rochechouart where Manet shows us the engraver Henri Guérard with his square beard and up-curled mustache, between, on his right, the model Ellen Andrée and, left, a young woman wearing a masculine-looking collar. It was to Guérard, who subsequently married Eva Gonzalès, that Manet presented the oval palette he had used when painting *Le bon Bock*, the picture with which he scored a popular success at the 1873 Salon. With the *Café*, *Place du Théâtre-Français* (1881), we are in the very heart of Paris.

Edouard Manet (1832-1883). Café, Place du Théâtre-Français, 1881.
Burrel Collection, Art Gallery, Glasgow.

Berthe Morisot (1841-1895). In the Bois, ca. 1881. Watercolor Drawing.
Cabinet des Dessins, Louvre, Paris.

Faintly tinged with bluish light, it is a Manet somewhat *à la Degas*. Now that his health was failing, he found pastels less exhausting than oils, and the *Café* was Manet's best production in this medium. The young woman with a tip-tilted nose watching the man who is smoking on the left (bisected by the frame in the Japanese manner) and the aproned waiter with his back to us compose a typically Parisian restaurant scene.

Like plants, cities sometimes feel a craving for fresh air and water; for trees and grassy meadows. In the days of the Impressionists Paris was conscious of a need for more breathing space and extending her domain along the banks and islands of the river. Our painters took part in this centrifugal movement and for a while the Seine became their favorite rendez-vous.

One of the "lungs" of Paris was the Bois de Boulogne whose avenues inspired Berthe Morisot, Mallarmé's friend, to some of her most charming pictures, rendered in tones hovering between green and blue and bathed in "delicately shimmering, silken light." "That word 'realist'," she wrote, "is nonsensical. Something of one's personality always creeps in, no matter how hard we try to be objective." And nothing could be more personal than this evocation of the Bois on a summer's day, with children playing on the grass and women strolling in the distance.

Further afield, from Saint-Cloud to Courbevoie, in the reaches between Suresnes, Asnières, Argenteuil and Bougival, the river was dotted with canoes and row-boats, while on Sunday afternoons those two picturesque little islands, La Jatte and La Grenouillère, were a favorite haunt of loving couples. And here was an atmosphere after our artists' hearts!

In this riverine setting Renoir now placed his figures—a habit he had developed since the early *Grenouillère* and *Boating at Chatou*. At Bougival "he grouped them round the tables of little country inns or set them dancing in couples." In *Dancing at Bougival* we see Suzanne Valadon walzing in the arms of

Auguste Renoir (1841-1919). Dancing at Bougival, 1883.
By Courtesy of the Museum of Fine Arts, Boston.

Paul Lhote who is in the typical get-up of the Parisian playing at rusticity. Wearing a simple cotton frock, the young woman is abandoning herself to the lilting strains of a small local band playing, likely as not, the then popular refrain, *Amanda*.

"Amanda," little Parisian seamstress, over-fond of carriage drives and dance-halls, has been happily personified by Renoir in this picture, her cheeks flushed with the excitement of the moment, superbly vital. Woman as Renoir depicts her "is a living entity, bodying forth—and how tellingly!—our love of life" [9].

Georges Seurat (1859-1891). Une Baignade, 1883-1884.
By Courtesy of the Trustees, Tate Gallery, London.

Then once again there came a change. Painters had quickly had their fill of sunshine, boating parties and the brief glamour of wind-ruffled streams. This quest of the quivering, ever-changing patterns of light which the season and the hour weave over stones and water, this tendency as it were to disintegrate nature, to reduce it to a haze of dancing atoms and treat reality as a mere pretext for variations on a charmingly elusive theme —all this was suspect to a younger generation. Returning to the studio, as to a place of refuge, these new men reaffirmed the prerogatives, of line, clean-cut forms and boldly stated planes.

It was in one of the nearer suburbs—at Asnières—that Seurat found the subject of his first picture on the grand scale, *Une Baignade*, but it was in his studio that he painted it. This canvas, for which he had made a great number of preliminary sketches on the spot, was painted, his friend Signac tells us, "in broad strokes brushed one over the other, with a palette of ochre and richly glowing tints. Like those of Delacroix, the colors were submerged in the 'patch'." And Signac goes on to define the characteristics of Seurat's art as follows: "Observation of the laws of contrast, a methodical separation of the picture elements (light, shade, local color, interactions of colors)" [10].

Saturated with summer heat, *Une Baignade* has an overall bluish hue. In the distance are factories with smoke rising from them through the still air. We are conscious of an emphasis on immobility; the light is heavier than the shadows. In an article in the magazine *Paris* Arsène Alexandre speaks of the great pains Seurat had taken to prepare himself for coping with this elaborately planned, large-scale work: his intensive studies (under Lehmann) at the Ecole des Beaux-Arts, and the little sketches he was always making as he roamed the streets of Paris, "perpetually drawing, trying to build up a language of his own, a very simple language, capable of recording swiftly but surely both outline and movement.

Georges Seurat (1859-1891). The Seine at Courbevoie, 1885.
Mme Cachin-Signac Collection, Paris.

"Then, when he had learnt, step by cautious step, all he had to know—like the raw recruit who learns how to march in the correct manner by having each of the movements explained to him (only Seurat had no corporal to instruct him)—he started putting his hard-won knowledge into practice and began

Georges Seurat (1859-1891). Suburban Scene, 1883.
Pierre Lévy Collection, Troyes.

by exhibiting *Une Baignade* at the Salon des Indépendants, rue Laffitte. Thereafter Seurat was the artist the younger men looked to for big effects; he was, it seemed, one of the few contemporaries capable of bringing off large-scale compositions, while using wholly original procedures" [11].

Next year—a year before the second landmark in his brief career, *Sunday Afternoon on the Island of La Grande Jatte*, that marvelous dialogue of sunlight and green shadows, with "a mixed Sunday crowd of Parisians enjoying a breath of country air" (Félix Fénéon), in which the dabs of color are given a new density and build up monumental form—Seurat produced a work of a boldness that took the public by surprise and heralded the triumph of "pointillism." Of relatively small dimensions this picture, *The Seine at Courbevoie*, has perhaps even more charm than any of the major works. What indeed could be more delightful than this glimpse of the river spangled with flecks of light, the woman walking her dog on the bank, the little sailboat moving in the opposite direction on the far side of the river, and the big tree in the foreground, one of those Italian poplars the faint incessant rustle of whose tiny leaves is so pleasant an accompaniment to a walk beside the Seine? Vibrant, limpid, memory-haunting, this is the most "musical" as well as the most sensitive of all the many views of suburban Paris that we owe to a French artist.

THE PARIS OF THE POST-IMPRESSIONISTS

MUCH has been said about the Impressionists but, so far anyhow, writers on art seem to have been chary of devoting equal attention to their immediate followers. The reason is, presumably, that success was slow in coming to the works produced by the group of men, almost all Parisians born, who formed the nucleus of the new movement.

Seurat, their leader, had all the traits of a man of science. "Picture a tall young man, extremely shy but full of indomitable energy; with the beard of an apostle and the gentleness of a girl; with a low, muted, persuasive voice; one of those quiet fanatics who may seem timid to a degree but actually shrink from nothing. Leading a cloistered, abstemious life in a small studio on the Boulevard de Clichy, he devoted himself heart and soul to his work—his industry was nothing short of prodigious— and spent what little money came his way (his means were of the slenderest) on costly technical experiments. At this time he was trying to demonstrate that his method of painting, while particularly appropriate to open-air subjects, could be applied also to big figures in interiors" [11].

The rejection of *Une Baignade* by the selection committee of the Salon in 1884, a year after Manet's death, speeded up the inauguration of the Salon des Indépendants (no selection committee and no prizes) in that year. Among its founders were Redon and Dubois-Pillet, in addition to Seurat and Signac. It was the latter, John Rewald tells us [12], who then initiated Seurat into the use of pure colors, juxtaposed in tiny dots.

Signac was an energetic young man with a gift for leadership and organization. Two of his canvases, *Pont d'Austerlitz* and *Rue Caulaincourt*, were hung beside his friend's big picture at the first exhibition of the Indépendants.

In 1885, at Guillaumin's studio, Signac made the acquaint-ance of Pissarro, to whom he introduced Seurat and of whom he made a convert to Divisionism. Sponsored by this old-guard Impressionist, Seurat and Signac (Dubois-Pillet having been contemptuously brushed aside by Degas) figured in the Eighth (and last) Impressionist Exhibition, which opened on May 15, 1886, in spacious rooms above the restaurant La Maison Dorée at the corner of Rue Laffitte and the Boulevard des Italiens.

Seurat's *Sunday Afternoon on the Grande Jatte* elicited ribald comments not only from the general public but even from some fellow artists. However he had his revenge in the June issue of *Vogue* which contained a glowing tribute by Fénéon to the new men. "Basic to Impressionism was a breaking-up of colors but this broken color was employed capriciously, unmethodi-cally; a streak of pigment drawn across a landscape produced a sensation of redness, while dabs of green were added to passages whose dominant tone was red. But Messrs Georges Seurat, Camille Pissarro, Dubois-Pillet and Paul Signac divide tones on scientific, well thought-out lines."

The group was in the habit of meeting in the Café d'Orient or the Café Marengo, and on Mondays at Signac's studio on the Boulevard de Clichy. All figured in the second Salon des Indé-pendants, held in a shop—painted blue—in the Rue Laffitte. "The fact that paper confetti were now being used in the mimic warfare of carnival," wrote Signac, "gave facetious critics a heaven-sent opportunity for making fun of us." And "confett-ists" was one of the epithets which—like "pointillists" and even "divisionists"—the new painters indignantly repudiated. Signac himself preferred to give the rather pedantic name of Chromo-luminarism to the new technique.

Signac had just produced *Two Milliners*, in which the impres-sion of space was conveyed in an ingenious way by the gesture of the woman bending forward to pick up her scissors fallen

Paul Signac (1863-1935). Two Milliners, 1885.
Émil Bührle Collection, Zurich.

on the floor. In a letter (August 1890) to Maurice de Beaubourg, Seurat singled out this picture—its setting was a milliner's workroom in the Rue du Caire in the heart of Paris—as being, along with *The Dining-Room*, his friend's best work.

Among Signac's various renderings of the Parisian scene mention may be made of his *Place Clichy*, which shows the

Paul Signac (1863-1935). The Dining-Room, 1886.
Kröller-Müller Museum, Otterlo.

famous square as it looked (and still looks) when invaded by a traveling fair. The painter's studio was just beside the statue of Marshal Moncey which figures in this picture.

The literary movement known as Symbolism was now in full swing in Paris and several of its leading lights championed the cause of the new painting. They had meetings at 79 Rue Blanche under the auspices of Félix Fénéon, editor of *La Revue Indé-pendante*, and contributed articles to *Vogue* and *L'Art Moderne*. Among the writers who, like Fénéon, took every opportunity of extolling the art of Signac and Seurat were Gustave Kahn, Paul Adam and Francis Viélé-Griffin; also Georges Lecomte, Huysmans and the Belgian poet Emile Verhaeren.

Patient, persistent and aggressive on occasion, Signac was the moving spirit of the Neo-Impressionists, and it was he who grouped together the various painters who—up to and including Cross—employed the pointillist technique. Among them were several who made a speciality of views of the Seine and its banks, one being the Parisian Albert Dubois-Pillet who held the rank of captain in the Garde Républicaine. With his bristling mustache and natty beard he looked a typical soldier—but art was his ruling passion. One of his early works was the *Dead Child*, a picture much admired by Zola, who even had it "repainted," so to speak, by one of the characters—Claude Lantier the artist—in one of his novels, in which he is described as having captured to perfection "the sheen of wintry sunlight as refracted by the ice crystals suspended in the frozen air." Among his best works are two riverscapes, *The Seine at Paris* and *The Seine at Bercy* (Puy Museum), showing "the low, flat river banks with the squat cylindrical mass of the Bastille in the offing and a reach of the river under a lucent dome of sky" [13].

Hayet, another Neo-Impressionist, was always something of a mystery man; some years later Signac completely failed to find out what had become of him. He had studied under Lucien,

Albert Dubois-Pillet (1846-1890). The Seine at Paris, 1888.
From the Collection of Mr and Mrs Arthur G. Altschul, New York.

Pissarro's eldest son, who counselled him to paint in dots of color; when doing his military service at Versailles, he showed his teacher a disk of 120 colors—the "spectrum palette" with a vengeance!—which he had made in barracks. In 1889 he painted his ingenious *Place de la Concorde*, showing the newly completed Eiffel Tower looming up behind the Obelisk.

What could be more Parisian than the Eiffel Tower? Two years before it reached completion a number of distinguished writers—amongst them Huysmans and François Coppée—had railed against this "dizzily grotesque erection towering above Paris like a huge black factory chimney" [14]. Huysmans saw in this "triumph" of industrial civilization "the pinnacle of a cheap-jack's Notre-Dame, a belfry without bells but fitted with a

Louis Hayet. Place de la Concorde, 1889.
Private Collection, New York.

Georges Seurat (1859-1891). The Eiffel Tower, 1889.
Collection of Mr and Mrs Germain Seligman, New York.

cannon to call the faithful to the Mass of High Finance, the brokers' vespers; a signal gun that booms a smoky summons to the cult of Capital" [15].

Seurat, however, who had a scientific turn of mind, seems to have been impressed by this feat of modern engineering; one of his pictures includes the Eiffel Tower, rising beyond the Pont d'Iéna into a sky dappled with vibrant brushstrokes. He often visited the public fairs at Neuilly and the Place du Trône, while showing an especial interest in those which took place only a few steps away from his room in the Boulevard de Clichy. Undeterred by the appalling din, he spent long hours

Georges Seurat (1859-1891). Le Chahut, 1889-1890.
Kröller-Müller Museum, Otterlo.

◄ Georges Seurat (1859-1891). La Parade, 1887-1888.
Stephen C. Clark Collection, New York.

making small preliminary notes of attitudes, gestures and sometimes even the painted decorations on the booths. Thus it was he sketched any number of *parades* (the outside shows given before performances in the booth) preparatory to his big picture, all in spangles like a Christmas tree, of the row of acrobats on their platform with a clown performing on the trombone and cornet-players wearing derbies. They form a horizontal strip of figures closed on the right by the man with a mustache, the showman who the moment the brass falls silent will launch into his patter. The same man figures in *Le Chahut*, where he has replaced his stick by the band-conductor's baton; then, whip in hand, directing the gyrations of the riders in *The Circus*.

For *Le Chahut*, finished in 1890, Seurat made—so Coquiot tells us—several studies in L'Ancien Monde, a popular café near the Boulevard de Clichy. When exhibited at Brussels, the picture was the target of violent attacks in the press, though acclaimed by Octave Maus and Emile Verhaeren. It was finally bought by Gustave Kahn [16]. The architecture of this picture is based on a counterpoint of horizontals and verticals, while "the sleek, black, parallel limbs of Seurat's capering puppets immortalize in their flashy way the 'folklore' of the eighties" [17].

From 1885 on Seurat frequented the Cirque Medrano, where he made countless sketches in tiny notebooks held in the palm of his hand. At this time he was hard at work on *The Circus*, that huge canvas in bright "Naples" yellow in which the dynamic movements of the galloping horse, the circus-rider and the clowns in the arena are so tellingly contrasted with the staid immobility of the spectators. He often worked at night, posted on a ladder, for he had arrived at so thorough an understanding of the properties of colors that, even when making do with artificial light, he knew exactly how they would look by daylight. He decided to exhibit *The Circus*, unfinished though it was, at the Salon des Indépendants. While seeing to the hanging of the picture he caught a quinsy of the throat and died three days later, on March 29, 1891, in his mother's house on the Boulevard de Magenta. Seurat's brief career as a painter—he was only 32 when he died—was one of absolute devotion to his art; "unexpansive, taciturn and an enigma even to his closest friends" [11], he had no outside interests in life.

On April 1, 1891, Pissarro wrote to his son Lucien, then in London: "Yesterday I went to Seurat's funeral. I saw Signac there; he was terribly cut up by his friend's death. I now think your opinion of Pointillism was right; it's played out."

Vincent van Gogh (1853-1890). View of Paris from the Butte Montmartre, 1886. Kunstmuseum, Basel.

A RAMBLE THROUGH PARIS

AND now, let us take a stroll through Paris as it was at the turn of the century, along streets that are nothing if not capricious, each with a personality, a whimsy of its own. Sometimes it scrambles up the "sacred hill," sometimes dives steeply to the boulevards, and sometimes, like Rue Berthe, hangs poised between earth and sky. And then again, we have majestic streets —all pomp and circumstance—like that spanning the capital from Père Lachaise to the Concorde.

Let us begin with the canvases Pissarro made in his studio when, from 1897 to 1899, after the break-up of the impressionist group, he painted a series of bird's-eye views of the Paris streets. Then in his late sixties, he was suffering from inflammation of the cornea and his state of health prevented him from doing long spells of work in the open.

Camille Pissarro (1830-1903). Rue d'Amsterdam, 1897.
Private Collection, Paris.

The Saint-Lazare station makes a good taking-off point for our excursion, and we shall begin by turning into the Rue d'Amsterdam which runs alongside the station and, like the Place de l'Europe under which the railway passes, gave in the spacious times of Charles X (1824-1830) on the estates of Messrs Hagermann and Mignon. To the dean of the Impressionists we owe a pleasantly vivacious representation of Rue d'Amsterdam; though it was rapidly executed in heavily charged brushstrokes, we can distinguish separately each of the passers-by. Next, following the Rue de Londres, we come to the Place de la Trinité, named after the "Trinitarians," the monks who officiated in the chapel of the old hospital of that name. Renoir painted it in 1890, as seen from the square now called Place Estienne d'Orves, when there still were horse-cabs drawn up alongside the railings of the square. Next, by the Rue de Chateaudun and the crossing known as the Carrefour des Ecrasés, owing to its perils for pedestrians, we reach the boulevards.

From this point up to the Opera, the Impressionists, headed by Pissarro, were in their element. One of the most delightful features of their art is what was styled the "pretext-landscape, a pictured fragment of nature charged with an autonomous vitality by small, flickering brushstrokes, and this technique they applied with like success to their street scenes, viewed in bird's-eye perspective from a window or balcony.

The Boulevard Montmartre, where we begin, is one of the most typically Parisian thoroughfares, with its cafés, its alleys, its multifarious shops and loitering crowds. Pissarro painted it as seen from his window in the Hôtel de Russie at the corner of Rue Drouot; a picture bathed in a sheen of pearly blue. "Just now," he wrote to his son on February 13, 1897, "I am getting some fine rain effects" [18]. The colors are suffused with silvery lights and through fluttering veils of leafage we glimpse the tides of traffic in the street below.

As we stroll towards the Opera, Pissarro shows us the Boulevards des Italiens, a riot of gay colors lit by the morning sun. We need only replace the two-decker buses by their modern equivalents, horse-cabs by taxis, and those quaint little Gothic edifices in wrought iron by the staid present-day conveniences shaped like metal containers, and we might almost take this for the Boulevard des Italiens of 1957.

A short walk in the direction of the Madeleine brings us to the Boulevard des Capucines, inaugurated in 1584 by Louise de Lorraine (wife of Henry III), whom we have mentioned as being present at the ball given for the Duke of Joyeuse. It was here, at the corner of the Rue Cambon, that on February 23 the 1848 revolution broke out. But let us pause for a moment in the stretch of boulevard between the Opera and the beginning of the Rue de la Chaussée-d'Antin, walk up to the fourth floor of the corner house and look down with Pissarro from the window on a gay profusion of blue, brown and black patches—the crowds thronging the sidewalk.

After a glance at the massive bulk of the Paris Opera and Carpeaux' statuary group ("Dancing") on its façade, we linger to admire the shop-windows in the Avenue de l'Opéra on our way to the Palais-Royal, where once more Pissarro is awaiting us. We are now at the beginning of 1898. While most of his friends were wintering in the country, at Giverny or Moret, or in the South of France, Pissarro, now aged 68, was given a commission by his dealer, Paul Durand-Ruel, for a series entitled *Avenue de l'Opéra*, celebrating that famous avenue, the luxurious shopping-center of fin-de-siècle Paris. He began by renting a room in the Hôtel du Louvre at the foot of the Avenue. "I have six canvases done and four on the stocks," he informed his son in a letter written at the end of February, "so you see I've not been wasting my time. I'd been reckoning a bit on Carnival, but the weather's atrocious, freezing; just now I can

Camille Pissarro (1830-1903). Boulevard Montmartre, 1897.
Sidney Brown Collection, Baden (Switzerland).

see a decorated float in the middle of the Avenue, but not a soul around." In May Durand-Ruel gave an exhibition of a dozen of the "Avenues" in a room specially reserved to Pissarro.

Next, in December, he rented an apartment at 204 Rue de Rivoli, "facing the Tuileries, with a splendid view of the gardens.

Camille Pissarro (1830-1903). Boulevard des Italiens, Morning, Sunlight, 1897. Chester Dale Collection, National Gallery of Art, Washington, D.C.

I have the Louvre on my left and, in the background, behind the trees, the houses on the Seine bank. On the right I can see the dome of the Invalides and the towers of Sainte Clotilde looming up behind clumps of chestnut trees. It's a lovely view and I see my way to making a fine series" [18].

Camille Pissarro (1830-1903). Avenue de l'Opéra, 1898.
The Minneapolis Institute of Arts.

By January 1899 he had moved on to the Tuileries, but
confined himself to recording effects of grey skies and rain.
He complained to his son of "the ear-splitting din" he had to put
up with in these vast gardens in the heart of the metropolis.
Meanwhile he possessed his soul in patience, "waiting for the
first leaves and flowers of Spring to put in an appearance."

Matisse remembered having met the aged painter at this time. "I knew him when he was staying in the Meurice, painting views of the Tuileries and the Rue de Rivoli. He was a very likable old fellow; with his patriarchal figure and hoary beard, he reminded me of one of the Prophets in Sluter's 'Well of Moses' at Dijon."

Another of Pissarro's homes was at 28 Place Dauphine, whence he had a view towards the Pont-Neuf. For two years, from the summer of 1900 on, the veteran painter, who had long since abandoned Divisionism and lost touch with his old friends,

Camille Pissarro (1830-1903). The Louvre and the Pont-Neuf, 1902.
Clark Art Institute, Williamstown (Mass.).

took this opportunity of exploring and exploiting "another of the picturesque bits of Paris." From his rooms he could watch the barges passing under the Pont des Arts. Jean Robiquet has described him working at one of his windows, wrapped in a warmly lined great-coat, an old man with a Father Christmas beard, and a kind, shrewd gaze. "His precarious health prevented him from painting out of doors, and one saw him at the window trying—with complete success—to conjure up on canvas one of the loveliest views in Paris, and by the same token all that remained to him of youth" [19].

And finally we reach the house at the junction of the boulevards Morland and Henri IV where he died, in November 1903, shortly after moving in.

Our ramble through the streets of Paris in the footsteps of the great Impressionist who loved them so well might be prolonged almost indefinitely. And always in his work we find the same subtle vibrancy of rapid, nervous strokes, of dancing colors, of tones placed seemingly haphazard, evocative of movement and the responses of an exquisitely receptive sensibility. "All is rendered in circumflex accents, comma-like flicks of the brush, streaks of red, green, blue and yellow, violet and lilac; here the tube has been squeezed and pigment heaped in tiny spirals; here the palette-knife has plastered the canvas like a wall; elsewhere it looks as if a bevy of sparrows had left their footprints in a dish of cream" [20].

LAUTREC'S AND BONNARD'S PARIS

IN his studio in the Rue Caulaincourt Toulouse-Lautrec had produced his early circus pictures about the time the Moulin Rouge first opened its doors. One of these, *The Circus Rider*, commissioned by Zidler, owner of the Moulin Rouge, hung for many years in the entrance of the famous dance hall. The model for the rider was Suzanne Valadon, one of Lautrec's neighbors, whom Degas called "the terrible Maria." At the time she had a small five year old son who later bore the name of Maurice Utrillo. Formerly an acrobat, she had ceased performing as the result of a trapeze accident.

Lautrec was a tirelessly acute observer of the Paris scene. In a previous volume in this series we have written of his "perambulations" in the Montmartre district, his interest in its nightlife and the human flotsam he encountered in its cafés. His physical infirmity was a link between him and these "outcasts," life's misfits, and in any case he had always had a predilection for all that lay beyond the barriers of convention. "For him," as one of his friends observed, "the world was not a gallery to be played to. He never thought that people were looking at him, it was he who looked at them, and all that went on around him was treasure trove for his eyes" [21].

The Moulin de la Galette and Moulin Rouge were his favorite hunting grounds—he could always count on meeting there the women he needed as models, among them Louise Weber, known as La Goulue, who had a genius for flamboyant vulgarity, and in particular Jane Avril, known as La Mélinite, a young floor-dancer of a very different stamp, all sophisticated, sylph-like charm. But he also painted the street-girls he met on his nocturnal prowls and the cartmen he saw crossing the Place Clichy, leading by the bridle their broken-down nags,

Henri de Toulouse-Lautrec (1864-1901). A First Communion, 1888.
Musée des Augustins, Toulouse.

Henri de Toulouse-Lautrec (1864-1901). Riding to the Bois, 1888.
By Courtesy of Dr Marjorie Lewisohn, New York.

in which he saw pathetic travesties of the thoroughbreds owned by his sportsman father, Count Alphonse de Toulouse-Lautrec, which figure in so many of his boyhood sketches.

To this gentleman-artist whom the ladies of the Pigalle district addressed as "Monsieur Henri" the châteaux in the South where he had spent his youth meant relatively little. He was Parisian to his skillful finger-tips, and we feel this in the witty crispness of his drawing, whether he is sketching bicycle races on the Buffalo cycle-track (a sport one of his *Revue Blanche* friends, Tristan Bernard, was actively promoting) or Père Forest's backyard gardens (headquarters of the Montmartre archery club and the setting of several of Lautrec's portraits) or making brilliantly effective posters for Yvette Guilbert and the *chansonniers*, most eminent of whom was Bruant. For all their unsparing precision, sometimes verging on caricature, we sense in Lautrec's drawings of living models a real kindliness and that respect for the human individual, no matter what his social status, which is rarely to be found outside Paris, where poverty has never been considered a disgrace.

Typically Parisian is the spirit of Lautrec's *First Communion*, a picture all in black and white, whose effect is due uniquely to a balanced distribution of the painted areas and the brownish hue of the cardboard support. In contrast with this scene located in one of the poorer districts of Paris (François Gauzi posed for the employee in his Sunday best who is pushing the perambulator), we have a scene of fashionable life, *Riding to the Bois*, a smartly dressed couple on horseback out for their morning canter in the park. Along with the *Trace-Horse of the Bus Line* and *The Washerwoman*, these formed part of a set of four illustrations Lautrec was commissioned to make for Emile Michelet's article *Summer at Paris* in *Paris Illustré* (July 7, 1888)

The article (at the foot of which the artist's name is not even mentioned) is dedicated to "the Parisians of the poorer class, who never go on holidays." For the "prolo," as the workingman then was called, seldom or never roamed beyond the limits of the old fortifications of the city. Not for him the sight of fields and woodlands and the only flowers he encountered as he tramped the busy streets were the roses wilting in flower-vendors' baskets and those quaintly vivid flowers of speech known as *fleurs du bitume*, the argot of the streets.

Gauzi has put on record [22] the singular fact that before giving him the *First Communion* Lautrec had offered the quartet of monochrome pictures published in *Paris Illustré* to Goupil, at 20 francs apiece! But he received the answer that, now these brush drawings had served their turn, there was no further use for them.

The end of Lautrec's Parisian career was a sad one, in the sanatorium in the Avenue de Madrid (at Neuilly) which his friend Dr Bourges had arranged for him to enter. For he was on the brink of a serious mental breakdown, due to alcoholic excess. He had even developed the dangerous habit of soaking the floor of his bedroom with kerosene so as to destroy the bugs he fancied he saw everywhere around him. Some weeks after he had entered what then was called "the madhouse," Jules Claretie wrote an article about him in *Le Journal*. "Lautrec is an odd type of man, by all accounts—like a character out of one of Hoffmann's tales: a grotesque little dwarf, with blubber lips, dragging around with him a portfolio almost as tall as himself. He has always been an eccentric, seeing only the macabre side of things and people, and he pictures living human beings like dead bodies laid out in the morgue" [23].

Lautrec was five years younger than Steinlen whom he must certainly have met at the Chat Noir or in the company of Bruant, of whom both artists have left us a number of portraits. Steinlen, who made a great name for himself with the subversive, somewhat anarchistic iconography of his black-and-white

Henri de Toulouse-Lautrec (1864-1901). Quadrille at the Moulin Rouge (detail), 1892. Chester Dale Collection, National Gallery of Art, Washington.

work—lithographs and drawings—had rooms in the Rue Caulaincourt. "He was usually to be seen dressed in a blue velvet jacket and blue trousers like those worn by carpenters" [24]. In his drawings and some oil paintings he stresses the gloomier

Henri de Toulouse-Lautrec (1864-1901). Monsieur Delaporte au "Jardin de Paris," 1893. Ny Carlsberg Glyptothek, Copenhagen.

aspects of Paris life: pale, emaciated girls—sisters of Charpentier's "Louise"— streaming out of the gloomy buildings where they toil, dark byways with wraith-like, sinister figures slinking beneath the infrequent street-lamps, their backs bowed, hands deep in their pockets, famished pilgrims of the night.

Steinlen worked for the anarchist periodical, *L'Assiette au Beurre*, run by a man named Schwarz, "cunningest, most commercial minded, most mercenary of all the paper-merchants of the day" [25], and put up with an unremunerative job because, as he said, "he felt it his duty to sacrifice something to Art and the Ideal."

But whereas Steinlen (like the Swiss artist Félix Vallotton) usually confined himself to black and white in his scenes of Paris life, another Parisian painter, Pierre Bonnard, was about to create rarer, subtler harmonies in orchestrating similar themes.

Born at Fontenay-aux-Roses, that charmingly named suburb just at the gates of Paris, Bonnard, after failing in the examination for an official post, took up decorative art as his profession. He added to his income by making color lithographs, posters and drawings for *La Revue Blanche*, the magazine which Thadée Natanson and his brother Alexandre had founded in October 1891 and which, thanks to the good offices of Félix Fénéon, championed the cause of "intelligent painters."

Finely conceived and no less finely rendered is the sequence of twelve lithographs, *Some Aspects of the Life of Paris* (1895), which complement in a fashion Lautrec's scenes of Parisian nightlife. Bonnard's Paris is a city of people who have been trapped and molded by the toilsome daily round and yet have kept their youth: the humble folk gravitating around Place Clichy, dressmakers' errand-girls, small shopkeepers and the like.

Commenting on his first one-man show (at Durand-Ruel's in 1896), Gustave Geffroy drew attention to the essentially Parisian

Pierre Bonnard (1867-1947). The Cab Horse, Boulevard des Batignolles, ca. 1895. Private Collection, New York.

qualities of his art. "The more one studies Bonnard's half-tints, the more closely one follows the course of those fluent lines, their swerves and clashes, the clearer it becomes that we have here an artist with a singularly gifted eye for the most significant traits in the incidents of Paris life, everyday or unusual, that are his favorite subjects... None has recorded more faithfully the

Pierre Bonnard (1867-1947). At the Moulin Rouge, 1896.
Wright Ludington Collection, Santa Barbara, California.

Pierre Bonnard (1867-1947). Paris, View by Night, 1900.
By Courtesy of Yale University Art Gallery, New Haven, Conn.

movements of children at play, the fragile grace of very young girls. A delightfully mobile line, of an almost simian agility, captures the ever-changing panorama of the streets and the most casual gestures of the people in them, aspects so transient and elusive as to be hardly noticed by the untrained eye" [26].

Rather like Verlaine (whose *Parallèlement* he illustrated) and like all Parisians born, Bonnard had no use for pomposity. He had an ironical turn of mind but never used it to humiliate; only the rich and eminent were targets of his sarcasm. One of the most attractive things about his paintings is their reflection of a temperament fundamentally kind and charitable. Bonnard had a very special tenderness for women, none of the scorn we often sense in Degas' handling of his models. He loved to paint the people in the street, the little workrooms in the Clignancourt district, the neighborhood shops on the ground floors of buildings, the streets running down from the Butte towards the boulevards, where the windows of the tall grimy houses, usually dirty, are shrouded in lackluster curtains. Sometimes he took a drive round his favorite districts in the yellow, wicker-seated vehicles of the old Paris Cab Company, "reeking of mildewed leather, mud-sodden carpets, wet dogs, polishing brushes and horse-sweat" [27].

Two of his most delightful works are *View from the Pont Royal*, in which we see the first green leaves of spring livening the bleakness of the quays, and a triptych showing the red wings of the "Mill of mills" viewed from a café across the street (the side panels represent supper parties). With his flickering, vibrant touches Bonnard conjured up, better perhaps than any other painter, the surreptitious glamour of Place Clichy by night, when women on the prowl are silhouetted, moth-like, for a moment against the garish light of cafés and shop-windows.

One of his friends was Alfred Jarry whose *Ubu Roi* (1895) delighted him so much that he made a number of small drawings inspired by its peculiar protagonist. Along with his brother-in-law Claude Terrasse and Jarry, Bonnard launched the Théâtre des Pantins (marionette theater), typically Parisian in its appeal to a small sophisticated public.

A description of it was given in the *Echo de Paris* of April 1, 1898. "At the back of a courtyard in the Rue Ballu is a Lilliputian theater made for the delectation of a select few. It was here that recently, with the aid of skillfully manipulated puppets, Alfred Jarry revived his *Ubu Roi*, that wild fantasia whose verbal outrages fell foul of squeamish ears on the occasion of its first

Pierre Bonnard (1867-1947). View of Paris from the Pont-Royal, ca. 1912.
Formerly Alfred Daber Collection, Paris.

Edouard Vuillard (1868-1940). The Park, 1898.
Collection of Mr and Mrs William B. Jaffe, New York.

performance at the Théâtre de l'Œuvre. The auditorium is small, but admirably decorated by Edouard Vuillard, with a firework display of colors, and by Pierre Bonnard with some black and grey figures treated with a fine bravura. Between curtains right and left, masking the wings, is a little box-stage like that of a Punch and Judy show, adorned with pictures that might have come out of an illustrated Rabelais" [28].

I doubt if Vuillard got as much amusement as Bonnard out of the Marionette Theater. They were of the same age and often worked together, but Vuillard was of a more serious turn of mind and had not his friend's boyish sense of fun. Until round about 1905 Bonnard and Vuillard produced a number of pictures of the more intimate aspects of Paris life, using the same neutral tones, the same "sensitive" nuances ("sensitive" was a fashionable word at the time, much as "anguished" is today), the same mat tempera colors.

Vuillard was then living in Square Vintimille (now Place Adolphe-Max) with his old mother, whom he adored and often painted. It was there I met him in 1925. He was a confirmed stay-at-home, wore an old-fashioned beard and deliberately posed as a proper-minded bourgeois. He had made many, too many concessions to academic standards and his work had lost its first fine rapture. Yet in his best period he had produced some wholly delightful scenes of family life as well as a number of outdoor scenes, one of which, *The Park*, is in its kind a masterpiece.

THE PARIS OF THE FAUVES

IT was in 1905, in Paris, that the Fauves acquired their name (meaning "wild beasts"). One of the leaders of the movement, Henri Matisse, has left an account of how its baptism took place. "At the Salon d'Automne all the canvases that had a bit of color were hung together in a big room, in the center of which was placed a group by Marque, a sculptor who specialized in amiable trifles in the best Renaissance spirit. This one showed some tiny children dancing—such charming little things! When everything was in place, Vauxcelles, the art critic, came into the room and no sooner did his eyes fall on Marque's piece than he exclaimed, 'What on earth is Donatello doing in this wild beasts' den?'—a quip that made art history."

There is no question that the pictures sent in by Matisse, Marquet, Derain, Vlaminck, Rouault, Valtat, Jean Puy and Manguin, hung in the "den" beside the Douanier Rousseau's *Hungry Lion*, were eminently calculated to shock the public of the day, so strident were their clashes of green and violet. Indeed even that discerning critic Gustave Geffroy was moved to comment on their "freakish colors."

However, though Fauvism's sensational début took place in 1905, there had been premonitory signs that art was heading this way. For among the progenitors of the Fauves may be counted Van Gogh, Gauguin and Seurat, the three artists who were the first to fuse together the small, scattered touches of Impressionism in broad planes of color.

Six years before, in his Corsican landscapes, Matisse had shown a tendency to indulge in ultra-vivid colors and slashing brushstrokes. Later, when he was working in Camillo's studio in the Rue de Rennes, where Eugène Carrière called in once a week to correct the students' work—Carrière did not, as some

Henri Matisse (1869-1954). Pont Saint-Michel, 1900.
W.A.N. Burden Collection, New York.

have thought, run an art school of his own—there was a general move among the younger men towards a brighter palette. "We came there," Matisse once told me, "simply to paint from the living model. We were not out to launch an attack on Carrière's style of painting; only we preferred to use bright, pure pigment instead of dull, washed-out colors."

Henri Matisse (1869-1954). A Glimpse of Notre-Dame in Late Afternoon, 1902. Albright Art Gallery, Buffalo, N.Y.

This was in 1899, and it was in this spirit and with a view to playing off the effect of the dark wall in the near foreground against the sunlit vista of the quaysides, bridges and buildings —rendered in broad, flat tracts of color—that Matisse painted the *Pont Saint-Michel* as seen from his studio window and made several views of Notre-Dame [29], sometimes in divisionist touches, sometimes in wide, synthetic planes. Dim, an almost spectral form, the great cathedral rises above the Seine whose bed is strongly hollowed out between the quays and under the arch of the Petit-Pont. Veiled in a violet-blue haze, the twin towers are evoked rather than depicted, the "picturesque" aspects of the scene being subordinated to the plastic organization of space and volumes.

"I was living then on the Quai Saint-Michel," Matisse tells us, "just above the premises of Vanier, Verlaine's publisher. My rooms were on the fifth floor and two of the windows over-looked the narrow arm of the Seine (between the Ile de la Cité and the Left Bank). A fine view, with Notre-Dame to the right, the Palais de Justice and the Préfecture on the left. Particularly lively was the spectacle on Sunday morning, with crowds of people nosing in the book-boxes lining the parapet... This was the very heart of Paris."

His little studio contained only an easel, a bed and a table on which were laid out the elements of a still life. Matisse often spent his evenings with his friend and neighbor Albert Marquet, a young man from Bordeaux with whom he had worked in Gustave Moreau's studio-school. The two friends used to paint together in the Luxembourg Gardens; it was there that Matisse made the small picture that he dedicated to Cross, and Marquet his view of the Luxembourg Palace with the ornamental lake in front, flanked by geraniums in vases.

Marquet showed even more interest than Matisse in the streets, quays, bridges and squares of the "City of cities" which had been his adopted home since he left Bordeaux at the age of fifteen. Paris, indeed, was Marquet's favorite theme. Encouraged by the author Charles-Louis Philippe, whose poetic vein of writing he admired, he made a set of illustrations for that romantic-realistic novel of Paris life, *Bubu de Montparnasse*— but the publisher turned them down. His renderings of the

Albert Marquet (1875-1947). The Pont-Neuf in Sunlight, 1906.
Boymans Museum, Rotterdam.

Albert Marquet (1875-1947). Notre-Dame, 1905.
Musée de Pau.

Albert Marquet (1875-1947). The Pont-Neuf, 1906.
Chester Dale Collection, National Gallery of Art, Washington, D. C.

Pont Saint-Michel were a sort of counterblast to Impressionism.
They are not a sequence of views of one and the same place
seen from the same angle and showing the changes of the
light according to the hour and the season of the year. Each
picture treats the motif in a different manner and has the breadth
of vision and monumentality characteristic of Fauve art—and

this despite a tendency to an ever mistier presentation. Another of Marquet's subjects was the Pont-Neuf, notably in his canvases of 1906. By then nothing remained of the bridge of the days of Tabarin or the Pont-Neuf of the close of the reign of Louis-Philippe, lined with the booths of booksellers, vendors of liquorice-water, clippers of dogs' coats and open-air kitchens. Marquet shows us the bridge bathed in sunlight, with the statue of Henry IV in the middle distance and the trees on the Vert Galant (promontory of the Ile de la Cité) in the background; the trees so eagerly watched by Parisians, year by year, for the first signs of spring's coming. In another canvas he gives us a bird's-eye view of the bridge, with its massive arches and roadway thronged with pedestrians, carts and carriages.

In his evocations of Paris Marquet often employs wide, simply treated planes, suffused with the pinkish glow given off by the ground under a faintly misted sun or veiled in the light vapors clinging to the river banks. Before his art had taken its definitive form, he made some most attractive renderings of Parisian avenues and monuments, even such unrewarding ones (from the painter's point of view) as the Madeleine.

Only brief mention can be made of Vlaminck's scenes of the Paris suburbs, with their stridences of yellows, reds and blues; of Louis Valtat's *The Seine and the Eiffel Tower*; of some early Dufys, such as the *Quai de l'Hôtel de Ville*, and *Mardi Gras Procession on the Boulevard Montmartre*, painted with those comma brushstrokes which in his *Fourteenth of July* were converted by Picasso into savage "claws," but in which there was as yet no hint of the impending cubist revolution.

Other Fauve painters have commemorated aspects of the Paris of fifty years ago. Braque (who at Collioure in the previous year had worked out a color scheme congenial to his vision) painted, about 1906, his *Canal Saint-Martin*. All is treated in large masses, violently colored in places and edged with blue;

79

the billowy clouds perhaps owe something to Boudin, but the rest is pure Braque. He shows us the canal with the tall buildings on the outskirts of the Villette district in the background. Beyond these begin the suburbs, those drab streets of ill-assorted houses, which Rouault has so often and so poignantly depicted in all their stark, pathetic ugliness.

Georges Braque (1882). Canal Saint-Martin, 1906.
Norbert Schimmel Collection, Great Neck, N. Y.

Georges Rouault (1871). The Suburbs, 1911.
Hahnloser Collection, Winterthur.

UTRILLO'S WALLS

"THEY say I paint in much the same way as Pissarro? Do you really think so?" This was a question that Utrillo often put to his drinking companions in the bistrots of Montmartre round about 1904. Were the answer "Yes," he was delighted. And in fact his painting at this time resembled that of Pissarro's pre-1870 period, when he was still under Corot's influence. Born on Christmas Day, 1883, when his mother was living in the Rue du Poteau in the heart of Montmartre, Utrillo was the first of our painters to invent a special palette for his Paris pictures. Not only did he employ an unusual range of colors —salmon-pinks, slightly vitriolic blues, warm blacks faintly flushed with carmine—but he had a gift for making them sing out against a background of white walls, for painting which he mixed real plaster of Paris (a product of the Montmartre soil) into his white.

White was Utrillo's speciality; one could almost say he had the same craving for it as for red wine. In his pictures of houses in the Rue des Saules or the Rue Saint-Rustique he gave it a rough, striated texture like that of their old, crumbling walls, while in those of "Berlioz' love-nest" and Mimi Pinson's home he plastered them with coat upon coat of white, not forgetting to reproduce the *graffiti*, lovers' hearts and so forth, scrawled on their pristine purity.

Utrillo was still using the rather muddy palette of his early days and heavily loaded brushstrokes à *la Monticelli* when he painted the Pont des Arts as seen from the Quai Malaquais. The bridge is shown in the middle distance under a sky of racing storm-clouds. This picture was one of the first of the views of Paris in which Utrillo (who then signed himself "Maurice U. Valadon") was to specialize, to such wonderful effect.

Maurice Utrillo (1883-1955). Quai Malaquais, 1906.
Paul Pétridès Collection, Paris.

Next we may turn to his *Rue Custine* (a street named after
a general beheaded in 1793), already charged with those tactile
values, that yeasty textural ferment, which was to be distinctive
of Utrillo's painting. On the richly worked impasto, palette-
knife, brush and fingers have left, successively, their imprints

Maurice Utrillo (1883-1955). Rue Custine, 1909.
Paul Pétridès Collection, Paris.

with the result that these many-hued walls seem not mere inert matter, but vibrant with a strange inner life.

In *Rue Drevet*—painted, like all Utrillo's views of Montmartre, with lover-like devotion—we find the same remarkable vitality. This street consists of the flight of steps formerly known as the "Trois-Frères" and a section of the Rue du Poirier now named Rue Berthe; Pierre Drevet was an engraver, among whose works were reproductions of portraits by Rigaud and Largillière. On the left of this still half-countrified corner of Paris we see the steps and wooded slopes leading up to the "Butte."

Maurice Utrillo (1883-1955). Rue Drevet, Montmartre, 1908.
Collection of Mr and Mrs Leigh B. Block, Chicago.

In the *Porte Saint-Martin* Utrillo's texture is even denser, and particularly effective is the perspective vista glimpsed through the arch of Bullet's monument (erected in 1674 to celebrate the glories of the Sun King's reign): the deep recession of that great artery of Paris, the Rue du Faubourg Saint-Martin.

Maurice Utrillo (1883-1955). Porte Saint-Martin, 1905-1910.
By Courtesy of the Trustees, Tate Gallery, London.

Following this street and Boulevard Magenta we climb once more the slope leading to Montmartre, and soon we are back in the heart of Utrillo's domain, in the Rue Chappe. This street owes its name to the inventor of the "optical telegraph," the physicist Claude Chappe, who set up one of his signal towers on the Butte. When painting this street, our artist, known to the denizens of the Place du Tertre by the odd nickname of "Maumau," planted his easel on the top floor of a building at the angle of the Rue Antoinette and the Rue des Trois-Frères. He shows us, viewed from high above, the street receding canyon-wise between blocks of houses, with a long flight of steps in the background.

Not far away we have the Rue des Abbesses, at a corner of which, abutting on the square, stands the peculiar church of that name with its vaguely octagonal tower. In the old days this street flanked the outbuildings of the Abbey of Montmartre founded in 1133 by Louis the Fat and his wife, Queen Adelaide. In 1792, under orders from a member of the Convention, Billaud-Varenne, the Abbey was evacuated, and some years later, confiscated by the State, was sold. It was at the shop of a picture-framer named Anzoli, situated at a corner of this square, that Utrillo exhibited his first canvas, and he made many pictures of the square, chiefly under snow. In the 1909 canvas we are shown the Rue des Abbesses, with a group of bystanders awaiting the end of a burial service.

And now we have before us the Sacré-Cœur, as we see it from the Place du Tertre, framed between walls of houses, when we are making our way to the old church of St Peter's, whose porch stands just in front. How skillfully Utrillo has brought out the contrast between the static masses of white stone and the upward thrust of the pediment, domes and crosses of the great basilica—a dialogue of doors and windows, roofs and cupolas, zones of blue and white!

Maurice Utrillo (1883-1955). Rue Chappe, 1912.
By Courtesy of Diana Esmond, New York.

Quite other than Utrillo's was the Paris where—in the Rue
des Martyrs and the Rue des Abbesses—Degas found the
models for his dancers; or the Paris of the Moulin de la Galette
dear to Renoir and the little shopgirls who climbed the hill of
Montmartre to waltz there in the heyday of Impressionism; or
Lautrec's Paris, that of the Moulin Rouge and scarlet nights,
of women dancing in a whirl of billowing skirts and ostrich-

plumes. Utrillo's Paris is a sort of backwater, a region of silent streets and housefronts like blank faces, that keep their secrets to themselves.

A time will come no doubt when some psychological-minded art-historian will seek to elicit the secrets so discreetly veiled behind the closed shutters of these stolid-looking houses. Utrillo's art is an invitation to roam the streets he knew and

Maurice Utrillo (1883-1955). Rue des Abbesses, 1909.
By Courtesy of John Hay Whitney, New York.

loved so well, but he has nothing explicit to tell us about the lives of those who dwelt behind their walls. His oeuvre is one long, colorful panorama of the district in which his lot was cast, its tortuous byways and time-scarred buildings. For him, as for Corot, stone was not dead matter but vibrant with a life of its own, and he brought to the painting of "exteriors" the sense of intimacy that others gave to "interiors".

Maurice Utrillo (1883-1955). St Peter's Church and the Sacré-Cœur seen from the Place du Tertre, 1910. Paul Pétridès Collection, Paris.

THE POET'S SUBURBS

UTRILLO was a simpleton. But even more simple-minded than he was the minor customs official at a toll-station just outside Paris who had become a familiar figure to the concierges of the Plaisance district taking the air on their doorsteps, as he walked by wearing a big black hat and always with something under his arm: a portfolio, a violin or a painter's box of colors. Henri Rousseau, the Douanier, typified in his innocently picturesque way the Paris of the small employee, the Paris whose little squares are crowded every Fourteenth of July with young men and women dancing to the strains of an accordion. He was not attracted by the Champs-Elysées; not for him the Bois de Boulogne and its showy turn-outs, and he only felt at home in the quieter working-class districts where windows are seldom opened except on Sundays.

In his works we have as it were a distillation of the very essence of the city, with its long rows of street-lamps, masts aligned beside the quays, gaunt factory-chimneys etched on the horizon—and an all-pervading atmosphere of homeliness. For Rousseau's art is at a far cry from Manet's "boulevards," from Lautrec's Moulin Rouge, or the frills and furbelows of *France-Champagne*. Deliberately ruling out those ephemeral aspects of the visible world which were the chief concern of the Impressionists, he looked beneath the surface, to the hard core of reality, with a vision as precise as it was sensitive. Thus he sees Paris as a fully integrated whole and in his evocations every touch has its significance. He shows us the Seine with its bridges, quays and tugboats; horse cabs rattling along the Quai d'Austerlitz, sand-carts on the foreshore of the Quai de Grenelle, or Parisians taking their ritual Sunday walk in tree-lined avenues or on the river banks.

Henri Rousseau (1844-1910). Notre-Dame, 1909.
The Phillips Collection, Washington, D.C.

Like most of Rousseau's paintings the *Toll-Gate* is somewhat difficult to date. As far back as 1885 he had sketched the revenue cutter attached to the riverine toll-station at the Quai d'Auteuil. He was fond of returning to the places where he had worked as a Douanier before retiring on a pension. This is a delightful

Henri Rousseau (1844-1910). Myself, Landscape Portrait, 1890.
National Gallery, Prague.

Henri Rousseau (1844-1910). The Toll-Gate, ca. 1900.
Samuel Courtauld Collection, London.

little canvas, with its soft tints of green, red-tiled houses, russet tints of early autumn, tiny patches of grass and light clouds drifting overhead. It calls up nostalgic memories of the Paris of my young days, of the toll-gates of Brancion and Gentilly, both of them particularly dear to Rousseau.

Henri Rousseau (1844-1910). Bois de Vincennes, 1901.
Private Collection, Basel.

His big "landscape-portrait" shows him standing, palette in hand, at a central point of the city with which he identified himself so lovingly; stationed like a watchman at his post on the Seine bank, near the Pont des Arts, where a boat is moored, bedecked with flags of all the nations of the world.

And in the figure of the artist with the big Latin-Quarter hat, in *Notre Dame* seen from Quai Henri IV, have we not the Douanier once more? He has halted on the river bank to admire the panoramic view of the dark bulk of the cathedral and the circular sweep of the buildings on the Ile Saint-Louis with their serried ranks of blue-black chimneys fretting a translucent sky.

Rousseau lived in the Rue Perrel in a cramped little room whose furnishings were of the scantiest: a plain deal table, three chairs, a wooden box and a truckle bed screened off by a flimsy curtain. He had a pension of a hundred francs a month which he eked out as best he could by giving drawing and music lessons in the intervals of painting pictures which sometimes made his flesh creep with their evocations of the forests of the night and their alarming fauna. But he had also a gift for depicting scenes of the city he knew so well, scenes of a poignant sincerity and simplicity, invested with that humble time-old poetry of the Parisian scene which found naïve expression in the street-songs and ballads of half a century ago. He had never lost his childhood sense of wonder and combined the fantastic and the real in his art with perfect naturalness. Some of his happiest pictures celebrate the simple recreations of the Paris working-class in their brief hours of leisure, strolling on Sunday afternoons in Parc Montsouris or fishing in the sunlit waters of the great river, immemorially dear to poets and lovers, that winds through the heart of Paris.

One of Rousseau's friends, the poet Guillaume Apollinaire, used to visit him accompanied by the young woman he called his "Muse," that charming artist Marie Laurencin. In the portrait

Marie Laurencin (1885-1956). Group of Artists (Picasso, Fernande Olivier, Apollinaire, Marie Laurencin), 1908. Cone Collection, The Baltimore Museum of Art.

group of artists now in the Cone Collection she shows us some of the Douanier's first admirers. On July 21 of the year this group was painted, Rousseau wrote to Guillaume: "I shall be delighted if you can come here Saturday evening and, as usual, regale us with some of your fine poems."

TRANSPOSITIONS OF PARIS

It was in Picasso's Rue Ravignan studio that the famous "Rousseau banquet" took place in 1908, two years before the Douanier's death. This studio was located in that ramshackle wooden building quaintly named the Bateau-Lavoir (after the boat wash-houses on the Seine), which was the birthplace of Cubism and headquarters of the international art that now had made its home in Paris.

Some have said it was at Horta de Ebro in Catalonia that Picasso made his first cubist pictures; others that he had already employed this technique when he was living at 130*ter* Boulevard de Clichy. Be this as it may, there is no question that it was at the Bateau-Lavoir in Montmartre that Picasso and his friends glimpsed, dimly perhaps as yet, the vast possibilities of the new esthetic. For none of these young artists had any wish to draw up a program or to lay down any sort of law; nor had they any clear idea of what this new approach to art might signify or the momentous destiny in store for it.

Let us try to picture the state of affairs in the art world when these young men rallied round Picasso. Since 1874, year of the First Impressionist Exhibition, painting had been tending to become a direct expression of the artist's response to visual actuality, and—until Seurat and Matisse appeared on the scene —organic unity and architecturally ordered structure had been relegated more and more into the background. Things had come to a point where all was expressed by color, seconded by sensitive, apparent, almost impromptu brushstrokes conveying the emotion of the man who, *qua* artist, invited us to share his immediate responses to the thing portrayed and the all-quickening potency of light. "When I'm in the dark," Claude Monet said, "I do not *think*."

So it is not surprising that a new generation of painters aimed at painting more deliberately—and at a distance from the motif—objects quite simple in themselves and almost geometrical in form, which would lend themselves to an art that did not "tell a story" and even had no obvious subject.

So far there was no question of wholly non-figurative painting, but even at this early stage nature imitation was reduced to what then seemed to be the minimum, with the result that more attention now was paid to esthetic values and to statement in purely plastic terms. Thus the subject of the picture ceased to be a factual image, which could be checked up so to speak with something in the visible world, but was the product of a complex of ideas and conscious cerebration—a self-denying ordinance reflected in the austerity of the early cubist palette.

Though relatively few in number, cubist representations of Paris give an excellent idea of the methods of this then so novel form of art, at once revolutionary and Cartesian: its tendency to abstract planes from the subject and to exhibit them in new arrangements and under aspects corresponding not to the retinal image but to the vision of the inner eye alone. The Cubist's aim, in short, was to record not the facts of visual experience, but the system of ideas they generated.

So far as I can ascertain, the first cubist pictures having Paris for their theme were two "views" of the *Sacré-Cœur*, one by Picasso (1909) which we are unable to trace, and another by Braque (1910). In the latter we see the cupola of the basilica, with its curves repeated several times above the roofs of houses. Braque followed this up with a view of rooftops (1911), in which the break with visual reality is more pronounced, the exact location of the scene being undetermined.

> *O mon silence ! Edifice dans l'âme,*
> *Mais comble d'or aux mille tuiles, Toit !*

Georges Braque (1882). The Sacré-Cœur, 1910. Private Collection, Roubaix.

There is indeed something in common between Paul Valéry's *Cimetière Marin* and the spirit of Braque's picture.

It might almost be described as a vision of the city and of space humanized and reconditioned, so to speak, by the imagination of the artist who arranges, as the fancy takes him, the slate roofs and chimneys which act at once as symbols of placid

Albert Gleizes (1881-1953). Bridges of Paris, 1912.
By Courtesy of the Sidney Janis Gallery, New York.

Fernand Léger (1881-1955). The Roofs, 1911.
Private Collection, New York.

domesticity and as taking-off points for flights of fancy. For behind these homely housetops, we glimpse an "insubstantial pageant" of towers and belfries rising against the sky.

We find the same synthetic vision in Albert Gleizes' *Bridges of Paris*. Some fragmentated elements can be recognized: stone arches, the superstructure of the Pont des Arts. But the general effect is one of a richly integrated whole: Paris and her river presented in a superbly orchestrated complex of overlapping planes.

After the Cubists proper, we may turn to Fernand Léger, whom Louis Vauxcelles wittily if rather unkindly styled a

Fernand Léger (1881-1955). Smoke over the Roofs, 1911.
By Courtesy of Putnam D. McMillan, Minneapolis.

"tubist"! In 1911 Léger painted *Roofs* and *Smoke over the Roofs* in a color scheme of tender blues and pinks, playing off fleecy wisps of smoke against the clean-cut angles of houses. "These quaint little puffs of smoke," said Guillaume Apollinaire, "might be an emblem of civilization and that crooked sky is the very sky above our streets."

In that year Léger had moved into no. 13 Rue de l'Ancienne Comédie after living in La Ruche for three years, sharing a studio with a friend. The building known as La Ruche, which owed its name ("the beehive") to its curious shape, was a sort of caravanserai for artists and political refugees. Penniless new-comers from far-off countries could count on finding there a room of sorts, without gas or sanitary conveniences, where they could bide their time and did not risk being turned into the street if they failed to pay their rent. (La Ruche still exists, at 2 Passage de Dantzig near the Vaugirard slaughterhouse.)

Many young men, destined to become leading lights of modern art, lived there in Léger's time. Amongst them were the Russian Archipenko who took up Cubism in 1908, the sculptors Lipchitz and Laurens and the painters Delaunay and Soutine (the latter has left us a picture of La Ruche which looks more like a landscape of White Russia). Max Jacob, Apollinaire, Reverdy and Blaise Cendrars resided at various times in this prolific if unsalubrious forcing-ground of aspiring genius, the last-named being its poet laureate. In one of his *Nineteen Elastic Poems*, composed in honor of Chagall, who came to live there in 1910, Cendrars describes the impressions of a visitor to La Ruche.

> *"Stairs, doors, more stairs*
> *And his door opens out like a newspaper,*
> *Covered with visiting-cards.*
> *Then closes, and one steps into chaos,*
> *Sheer, rampageous disorder!"*

Léger was a happy man in the sense that he enjoyed the age that he lived in. I can still remember what he said to me one evening over a café table: "Oh boy, it's good to be alive! We moderns register a hundred times more impressions every day than any of your 18th-century artists!"

Lastly we may mention a late-comer to the cubist fold (in which Léger almost cut the figure of a "deviationist"): Juan Gris. When in 1912 he painted *Houses in Paris* he had not as yet achieved a balance between the two art languages, figurative and non-figurative, as he did later in *Place Ravignan*, which might have been subtitled: View from my window. "I am now trying," he wrote to a friend, "to rid my painting of all that is too crudely realistic. As a result, if I may say so, it has become more poetic. I hope to be able to succeed in expressing, with complete accuracy and with elements of a purely mental order, an *imagined* reality. In short to produce paintings that are precise and inexact, the opposite of bad painting, which is exact and imprecise" [30].

Such was the Paris of the Cubists in that brief golden age before the first World War. True, since the days of the Romantic movement Paris had been a lodestone for aspiring artists, but never before to this extent. You now could see men and women from all countries of the world rubbing shoulders around the marble-topped tables of the Montparnasse cafés and it was when the new-comers were thronging to this part of Paris and our young "Montparnos" making history that Apollinaire published his famous work *The Cubist Painters*. Under his auspices, the Closerie des Lilas became the leading literary and artistic café of the Left Bank, patronized by Futurists, Cubists and all the *avant-garde*.

"Montparnasse," he wrote, "has ousted Montmartre. Our artists, alpinists born, have migrated from one Mount to another; for art lives always on the heights."

★

O<small>N MAY</small> 1, 1900, opening day of the World's Fair, Parisians discovered that a new city, the city of a dream, had sprung up in their midst almost overnight. All but the most reactionary-minded were delighted with the green vistas of the avenues converging on the Pont Alexandre III, finest of Parisian bridges (its foundation stone had been laid by Czar Nicholas II in 1896), with the "Palaces of the Nations" along the riverside, the gardens of the Champ-de-Mars and the exotic pavilions grouped around the Trocadéro.

The beginning of the 20th century found Paris in an optimistic mood. The city had now its subway and the young republic, with typically French resilience, had made a spectacular recovery from the depression following the débâcle of 1870. The Fair was hailed as an emblem of the new era of peace and plenty that was beginning under the firm but kindly auspices of President Loubet.

So far as art was concerned, however, the space allotted to the Impressionists—still regarded with suspicion in many quarters—was sadly meager. "On visiting this bright, well-lit little room," wrote André Mellerio, "one cannot but be delighted with what one sees there. Only—how much is missing!" [31]

The vogue was then for the opalescent, blue-green hues of fin-de-siècle art; for "trailing convolvuli, tall gladioli, drowsy poppies, sinuous, faintly sinister water-plants, flowers with languorously drooping petals" [32]. In this tangled luxuriance of sea-weed and lianas, the euphoniously named beauties of the day, Cléo de Mérode, Liane de Pougy, Emilienne d'Alençon played their decorative parts and all Paris flocked to hear the golden voice of Sarah Bernhardt. And Parisians were no less quick to adopt the "slightly abnormal orphan" fathered on them by Monsieur Gustave Eiffel.

Robert Delaunay (1885-1941). The Eiffel Tower, 1911.
By Courtesy of The Solomon R. Guggenheim Museum, New York.

Once it had become a familiar feature of the landscape, the Tower played the part for painters of a gigantic still life set up in the very heart of Paris, and thanks to its immense height (984 ft.) every artist—Fauve, Cubist, Futurist or Nabi—no matter the district in which he lived, had it constantly before his eyes.

We have already seen the Tower as Seurat painted it at the time of the 1889 World's Fair when it had just been inaugurated. The Douanier Rousseau showed it soaring up above a clump of trees, and it became the pet preserve, as it were, of one of his friends, Robert Delaunay. For Delaunay, too, specialized in views of Paris; of its windows, of the pointed arches of Saint-Séverin, and above all of the Eiffel Tower. In so far as his work consisted of concrete images, things existing in the real world—fragments of curtains, the Paris streets, the Eiffel Tower—he played the part of an heresiarch of Cubism, using a syntax of what he styled "simultaneous contrasts." "Some people accused me," he once told me, "of harking back to Impressionism. Fortunately Apollinaire came to my rescue when he gave my method, a sort of spread-eagled Cubism, the name of 'Orphism'."

The Tower was likened to "a tall young lady doing the splits" and Delaunay pictured her in all sorts of postures, before he took to an increasingly non-figurative mode of expression. His first picture of the Tower bears an inscription in his hand: *Movement, Depth, 1909, France-Russia*. Then came the one we reproduce, where well placed curves are skillfully contrasted with the verticals of the tower itself, in a cataract of convolutions. The color scheme—of browns and full-bodied reds telling out against blue-greys and white—is purely arbitrary. The Tower appears, reiterated *ad infinitum*, in the center of *Simultaneous Windows* (1912); also, caught in a yet more convoluted and convulsive movement, in *Sun and Tower* (1913); and yet again, alongside the Big Wheel, in *The Three Windows* (1914).

Jean Bazaine (1904). Child on the Banks of the Seine, 1946.
Galerie Louis Carré, Paris.

Marcel Gromaire (1892). The Fourteenth of July, 1956.
Louis Carré Collection, Paris.

Some ten years later (in 1925), in his allegorical figures of the City of Paris, Delaunay handled the subject on very different lines, approximating to the decorative treatment of the same theme by Pierre Bonnard, his senior by 18 years.

In 1918 Bonnard had found in the Eiffel Tower a pretext for breaking away from his familiar round of the streets and sights of Montmartre. The spectator is standing on the Quai d'Auteuil (now Quai Louis Blériot), with the Pont de Grenelle in front and, rising above the Ile aux Cygnes, the replica of Bartholdi's Statue of Liberty. With its slightly acid colors, green and a purplish-blue flushing into orange, and with its throbbing light—a subtle, all-pervading vibration laced with sudden glints and transparences—this picture (reproduced on the jacket) has something of the magical quality of Debussy's music.

Chagall has shown us lovers embracing in the shadows of the tower, and in his ballet *Les Mariés de la Tour Eiffel* (1921) Jean Cocteau gave the same setting to the newlyweds performing a ritual dance between two gramophones. We have Utrillo's Tower glimpsed from one of those interminable streets so characteristic of the *banlieue*; and André Lhote's, seen through the smoke rising from tugboats on the river. Gromaire, too, has shown us the Tower aureoled in a white blaze of light behind one of the bandstands set up in the streets of Paris on the Fourteenth of July.

More ingenious is Dufy's rendering of the Eiffel Tower under the slim crescent of a young moon in the heart of a city vibrant with strange enchantments, glints of shimmering blue. Under a starry sky is what looks like a haphazard jumble of the ideograms that are the hallmark of our painter-magician's art: tiny squares, triangles, loops, comma-like strokes and dots. But we need only step back and all falls into place: houses, roofs, domes, the familiar buildings on both sides of the Seine, avenues of trees quivering in the nightbreeze.

Perhaps, indeed, it is by night that the Tower looks its best and thus that we visualize it, now it has won its place among our "ancient monuments" and ceased to be regarded as a robot interloper. Léon-Paul Fargue, most Parisian of poets, whose death ten years ago was an irreparable loss to French literature, has conveyed this idea with characteristic verve.

"In my young days when the tower had lately risen from the ground, like a quadruped with its legs splayed out, our esthetes scoffed at it. Later, when it had become a landmark and was taken seriously, intellectuals with an itch to poetize sat up and looked at it. The Tower was accepted in high society, introduced to gentlemen with monocles, made much of in books on Paris. Today it is hardly noticed—taken for granted. Only on chinaware and souvenirs de Paris does it catch the eye like an audacious not to say outrageous diadem on the headdress of a great capital city.

"Spinal column of a skyscraper, it can be seen from attic windows, from trains speeding back to the ants' nests of Montmartre, Saint-Cloud, the Champs-Elysées—this sky-aspiring, steely-blue Venus whose whisperings creep night and day into our radios.

"And night-long when the eyelids of the stations have closed upon the rails and our shadows are submerged by millions underneath the sheets . . . the Tower soars through the darkness as if aspiring to hitch Paris to a star" [33].

★

WE now have reached the penultimate phase of our subject, those paintings of some ten years ago, in which the presence of Paris is still conveyed by some suggestive detail —pending the most recent phase, the art of the fifties, in which identifiable elements are refined almost out of recognition.

Marc Chagall (1887). Sunday, 1952-1954.
Private Collection, Paris.

To that penultimate phase belongs Bazaine's *Child on the Banks of the Seine* (1946) in which once more we glimpse the Eiffel Tower. This canvas has quite definite associations for the painter. "It's a recall," he once told me, "of the walks I used to take with my little daughter—she was two or three at the time—in the Champ-de-Mars and along the Seine, in that magical light peculiar to the Ile-de-France. I hadn't yet broken with external forms, that's to say outlines, and was trying to confront (sometimes to integrate) very different or even incompatible structures: a child, a landscape, the Eiffel Tower."

From now on we have to grope our way in that labyrinth of poetic fancies in which Paul Klee played the part of an amiable Minotaur. As far back as 1921 he painted cities on these lines —though Paris was not one of them—and the idea behind his townscapes was quite other than that which inspired the carefully elaborated, more or less synthetic compositions produced by such men, different though they are, as Picasso, Beaudin and Fernand Dubuis.

It was just after the dark days of the German occupation that in his studio in Rue des Grands-Augustins Picasso painted "his" Paris, all in tones of blue, brown and grey. In a sequence of small, compact, somewhat cryptic compositions he recorded the essential aspects of the city—as if seen in the far distance from a high window: the towers of Notre-Dame, arches of the bridges, the Sacré-Cœur shining in the darkness as if a searchlight were playing on it.

In Beaudin's views of the Seine the synthesis is of a different order, no longer austere but charged with sensitive poetic feeling. The buildings rising above the river seem no more than patches of tinted shadows, but so precise is the line that we recognize them at once: the houses on the Ile Saint-Louis, the Conciergerie, the Louvre. One might almost take them for the working drawings of a professional engineer with

Pablo Picasso (1881). View of Paris, 1944-1945. Private Collection, Paris.

an artistic temperament who has enlivened his diagrams with bands of various colors, pink and yellow lamp-globes.

Henceforth artists tend to evoke Paris by indirection, but also with an eye to all that is most constant and most cherished in the aspects of our city: well-balanced proportions, a special light and infinitely subtle color harmonies.

Nicolas de Staël (1914-1955). The Roofs of Paris, 1952.
Musée d'Art Moderne, Paris.

It was in this spirit that Nicolas de Staël painted the roofs of the Rue Gauguet as seen from his studio in that district of building contractors whose workyards overhang the Avenue du Parc Montsouris. While rejecting all trick effects however brilliant, he manipulated texture, light and tone with a virtuosity that matched his fervid vision and his quest of an absolute in the chaos of appearances. "It's hard to get these roofs just as I want them," he once told me. "I am out to capture what's essentially organic and may serve as a solid starting-off point for my future work." And he swept with his gaze the broad vista of low roofs seen from his window. This is what he shows us in the canvas now in the Musée d'Art Moderne.

Somehow I picture him holding to his ear a seashell murmurous with the sounds of traffic far below, as he gazes down at the checkerwork of blue and greyish squares, sometimes red-rimmed and broken here and there with gleams of silvery white, under a vast expanse of sky. That murmur, "which," Valéry said, "is always in my ears, an ever-rolling river telling of the presence, the same yet constantly renewed, of the great city; a steady rumble alive with movements which I come back to and consult in the interval between two ideas".[34]

None the less—and this is yet another proof that the continuity of tradition, in the best sense, is ensured by experiments and innovations that, at the moment, may seem ill-advised—are we not justified in regarding this work by Staël as a companion piece to the painting by Van Gogh reproduced earlier in this volume? When I compare Van Gogh's Montmartre and Nicolas de Staël's Montsouris (nor must we forget that these are the two highest points of Paris), I am amazed to find they have so much in common. Despite the changes that have come over methods of expression, the emotion behind these pictures is that of two kindred spirits—destined, moreover, to come to the same tragic end at almost the same age.

And, when all is said and done, should this surprise us? All these works are products of the same soil, fruits of the same tree. When I examine the new lyricism of contemporary French artists and what our pundits call their "crazy optics," and even the works being produced in present-day Paris in which the

Maria-Helena Vieira da Silva (1908). Saint Lazare Station, 1949. Galerie Jeanne Bucher, Paris.

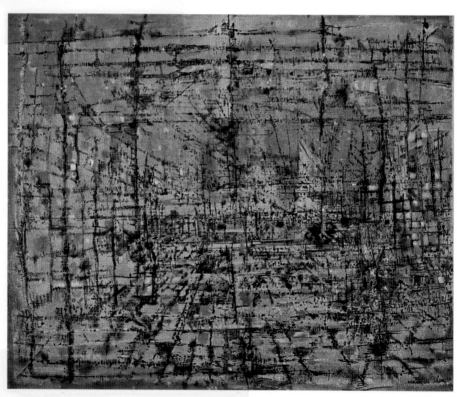

thing seen, the retinal image, is changed out of recognition in compositions that may seem (though this is not the case) deliberately contrived to baffle the beholder—when I examine this new art, a host of memories flicker into my mind, memories of our history-laden past. I seem to see the Paris of the Sainte-Chapelle where under the arcades designed by Jean de Montreuil, Saint Louis' architect, resounded the motets of Guillaume de Machaut; the long, winding cortèges Fouquet so well conjures up before us; the Paris of the "huntresses" whom Francis I kept waiting for him in the inns; the Paris of the Place Royale (now Place des Vosges), the Rue Saint-Jacques and the banks of the Seine with their crowds of tiny figures in gaily plumed hats; the Pont Notre-Dame and Gersaint's picture-shop; the Paris of the "enlightenment," the Paris dressed up à *l'orientale* in those mad, glad years before the war-songs of the revolutionaries echoed in the streets.

Then, coming nearer to our time, I conjure up mental pictures of the Palais-Royal in the heyday of the Directoire, the studios of David and Delacroix, the Cité in Meryon's time, Daumier's Ile Saint-Louis, the motley crowds of the World's Fairs, Manet's Paris and the boulevards as Renoir, Monet and Pissarro saw them in a haze of dancing flecks of color; urban and suburban Paris; the ballets at the Opera, boating-parties on the Seine, and the Eiffel Tower at the turn of the century when it was still the cynosure of Parisians and visitors alike. And in all these visions of our city's past, dead and done with in appearance, I seem to discern secret intimations of the Paris of today and of tomorrow, fraught with memories of times when fortune frowned and *le gai Paris* was in the doldrums, yet capable at any moment of rejuvenation, of springing on us some new and ravishing surprise and becoming once again the young Lutetia cradled in the Cité, that inviolate island whose citizenship is open to all the world.

André Beaudin (1895). Pont du Louvre, 1956.
Alfred Richet Collection, Paris.

The armorial bearings of the City of Paris represent a galleon in full sail accompanied by the motto Fluctuat nec mergitur, *and what device could be more fitting for a city that, buffeted by many a storm —siege, revolution, famine, enemy occupation—has "never foundered" and preserved its personality so gallantly intact for some two thousand years? A personality strongly molded by tradition, yet capable of the most daring ventures ; skeptical yet idealistic ; logical through and through in its approach to life, yet singularly intrepid in its flights of fancy. For the spirit of Paris, as reflected in its literature and visual arts, is the same "spirit of enquiry" as that to which the literature and art of Athens owe their indefeasible pre-eminence.*

One of the characteristics of our modern culture is the large part played in it by the visible—we are a generation of "sight-seers" in the best and worthiest sense—and nowadays in many fields the eye has stolen a march on other organs of perception. And is it not in Paris that the taste of our time is shaped and fashions are launched, that artists of all nations forgather and the painting of tomorrow forever takes its rise ? The Parisian eye, it has been said and rightly said, "is at once the most inquisitive and the most sophisticated organ of sight that the world has known since the age of classical antiquity."

"A hard-working old man" was Baudelaire's description of Paris. Hard-working, yes, but if old in years perennially young in temperament. And it is thus that I visualize the city where I live ; always ready to be up-and-doing, to bring off some miracle of rejuvenation, like the street-cleaner I see in early morning, setting loose along the sidewalk a purifying stream of clean, sparkling water, to flush away the débris accumulated in the gutters of our ancient streets.

NOTES AND REFERENCES

★

SELECTED BIBLIOGRAPHY
INDEX OF NAMES
LIST OF COLORPLATES
CONTENTS

NOTES AND REFERENCES

[1] Baudelaire, *Salon de 1846, Des écoles et des ouvriers*, in *Curiosités Esthétiques*. In 1855, year of the first World's Fair, Baudelaire had foreseen the coming of the new art, in which the old traditions went by the board, and of the independent "modern" artist.

[2] Edmond de Goncourt, *Journal*, 1871.

[3] Edmond and Jules de Goncourt, *Manette Salomon*, 1866. Actually, though Crescent had all the makings of an Impressionist, the Goncourts saw in him a painter of the Barbizon School. *Vide* Erich Koehler, *Edmond und Jules de Goncourt, Die Begründer des Impressionismus*, Leipzig 1912.

[4] Armand Silvestre, *Au pays des souvenirs (Le Café Guerbois)*, Paris 1892. Silvestre names among the habitués of the Guerbois: Manet, Duranty, Zola, Desboutins, Hippolyte Babou and Fantin-Latour.

[5] George Moore, *Confessions of a Young Man*, London 1888.

[6] Gustave Geffroy, *Renoir*, in *Le Journal*, March 6, 1896. M. Jean Adhémar, Curator of the Département des Estampes at the Bibliothèque Nationale, has kindly drawn our attention to this passage; also to some other articles by Geffroy and Arsène Alexandre quoted in the present work.

[7] Félix Fénéon, *Les Impressionnistes en 1886*, Paris 1886. A brilliant, if unprolific, writer and an exceptionally enlightened critic, Fénéon did much to further the neo-impressionist movement. He contributed to anarchist papers but, according to those who knew him best, his anarchism was largely an esthetic affectation. However, he figured in the trial known in France as the *Procès des Trente*. When the judge accused him of "being seen talking to an anarchist behind a street-lamp," Fénéon could not resist a Wildean rejoinder: "And might I ask Your Honor what exactly is the 'behind' of a street-lamp?"

[8] *Lettres de Degas*, collected and annotated by Marcel Guérin, preface by Daniel Halévy, Grasset, Paris 1945.

[9] J. C. Holl, *Après l'Impressionnisme*, Paris 1910. "Art today seems to be going cosmopolitan," observes M. Holl somewhat regretfully. But surely that was quite natural when he wrote; the times had changed.

[10] Paul Signac, *Préface au Catalogue de l'Exposition Seurat et ses amis*, Galerie des Beaux-Arts, December 1933-January 1934. This preface quotes the description of his technique dictated by Seurat to Jules Christophe.

"Art is harmony; harmony is an analogy of contraries (contrasts) and an analogy of similarities (shadings) of tones, colors and lines. Tone here means light and shade; color, the use of complementaries (red-green, orange-blue, yellow-violet); line means bearings taken on the horizontal. These various harmonies can be calm, gay or sad; gaiety of tone is caused by a luminous dominant; of color, by a warm dominant; of line, by lines ascending from the horizontal. Calmness of tone is caused by an equality of darks and lights, of warm and cool tints, and by horizontal lines . . . The means of expression is the optical mixture of tones and colors, and of their reactions (shadows), according to absolutely fixed rules."

[11] Arsène Alexandre, *Seurat*, in Paris, April 1, 1891. He adds: "The *Grande Jatte* inaugurated his second phase and it shocked the public. In this big canvas everything was new: the boldness of its whole conception and the extraordinary nature of the technique—this much-talked-of 'pointillism'."

[12] John Rewald, *Post-Impressionism, From Van Gogh to Gauguin*, New York 1956, published by the Museum of Modern Art. It is the most complete study of Post-Impressionism that so far exists.

[13] *Petit glossaire pour servir à l'intelligence des auteurs décadents*, by Jacques Flowert, Vanier, Paris 1888. From a note written by Fénéon on a copy now in the Bibliothèque Nationale we learn that "Monsieur F.F." was one of the compilers of this glossary. In the *Petit Bottin des Lettres et des Arts* (Giraud, Paris 1886) we find a reference to Dubois-Pillet. "Captain and Impressionist. Eyeglass. Handsome beard and stiff mustache. Flowers, landscapes, portraits, people. Has a knack of catching the glints of wintry sunlight refracted by ice-crystals present in the frozen air, and is proud of it." The (unnamed) authors of the *Petit Bottin* were Paul Adam, Oscar Méténier, Jean Moréas and Félix Fénéon.

[14] Protest addressed to M. Alphand, president of the committee sponsoring the Tower (*Eiffel*, Jean Prévost, Rieder, Paris 1929).

[15] Joris-Karl Huysmans, *Certains*, Tresse and Stock, Paris 1889.

[16] Seurat sold two canvases in his lifetime: *Le Chahut* and another, in 1887, at an exhibition of "Les Vingt" organized by that perspicacious connoisseur Octave Maus at Brussels.

[17] André Salmon, *Propos d'atelier (La révélation de Seurat)*, Crès, 1922.

[18] Pissarro, *Lettres à son fils*, edited by John Rewald, Albin Michel, Paris 1950.

[19] Jean Robiquet, *L'Impressionnisme vécu*, Julliard, Paris 1948.
M. Robiquet seems to have made some errors as regards the dates of Pissarro's last residences in Paris. We have corrected these in the light of the painter's correspondence.

[20] André Michel, *Pissarro*, in *Le Journal des Débats*, March 16, 1893. The author adds: "I never visit our Bibliothèque Nationale without regretting, during the tedious hours when I am waiting for the books I want to read, the fact that neither Pissarro nor Monet was called in to decorate the upper panels where now we see a mass of undulating tree-tops. What refreshing glimpses of sun and sky and nature they would have conjured up before our waiting eyes!"

[21] Tristan Bernard, *Préface au Catalogue de l'Exposition des œuvres de Toulouse-Lautrec*, at the Pavillon de Marsan, Paris 1931.

[22] François Gauzi, *Souvenirs sur Toulouse-Lautrec*, David Perret, Bibliothèque des Arts, Paris 1954. Gauzi was born in 1862 in the Haut-Languedoc province. Himself a painter, he had met Lautrec in Cormon's studio. He figures in two of Lautrec's canvases and in several drawings.

[23] Jules Claretie, *Le Journal*, March 22, 1899.

[24] Jules Renard, *Le Journal*, June 14, 1899.

[25] Letter from Steinlen to Nadar. Holograph, Bibliothèque Nationale, Paris.

[26] Gustave Geffroy, *Bonnard*, in *Le Journal*, January 8, 1896, with reference to the painter's first one-man show (pictures, posters, lithographs) at Durand-Ruel's gallery.

[27] Léon-Paul Fargue, *D'après Paris (Le Fiacre)*. He thus describes the cabman: "Putty-colored great-coat with flat metal buttons, glossy white top-hat looking like a big blancmange."

[28] This article is signed: *La Cagoule* (the cowl).

[29] In *A Glimpse of Notre-Dame in Late Afternoon* at the Albright Art Gallery, Buffalo, N.Y., though the shape of the building is simplified to an extreme, nothing of its actuality is scamped. "You have often been reproached, my dear Matisse," wrote Guillaume Apollinaire, "for this summary method of expression. They don't realize that you have brought off one of the most difficult feats, that of bringing the subjects of your pictures to plastic life without having recourse to the 'object' except as a means of stimulating our sensations."

[30] Juan Gris' letter was reproduced in facsimile in the catalogue of the Juan Gris Exhibition, Buchholz Gallery, New York, January-February 1950.

[31] André Mellerio, *Les Impressionnistes à l'Exposition Universelle de 1900*, Floury, Paris 1900. The exhibits consisted of "some early landscapes by Monet, Pissarro and Sisley; almost all Renoir's figure pieces except *The Box at the Theater* and *The Dancer*; two canvases and three or four pastels by Degas; a few Cézannes, very few Berthe Morisots, one Guillaumin, some Boudins here and there—a rather meager showing."

[32] Louis Chéronnet, *Paris vers 1900*, Chroniques du Jour, Paris 1932. We can warmly recommend this excellent work by a friend of ours, who knew his Paris well.

[33] Léon-Paul Fargue, *La Tour Eiffel*, special issue of *La Renaissance* (June 1939) commemorating the Tower's fiftieth anniversary.

[34] Paul Valéry, *Présence de Paris*, Paris [1940].

SELECTED BIBLIOGRAPHY

Adolphe BERTY, *Histoire générale de Paris*, Imprimerie Nationale, Paris, 8 vols. — *Paris Guide*, with contributions by the leading artists and writers of France, Lacroix, Paris 1867, 2 vols. — Abbé LEBEUF, *Histoire de la ville et du diocèse de Paris*, Féchoz, Paris 1883, 7 vols. — F. HOFFBAUER, *Paris à travers les âges, aspects successifs des monuments et quartiers historiques de Paris, du XIIIe siècle à 1885*, Firmin Didot, Paris 1885, 2 vols. — Armand SILVESTRE, *Au pays des souvenirs*, Paris 1892. — Gustave PESSARD, *Nouveau dictionnaire historique de Paris*, Eugène Rey, Paris 1904. — Karl SCHEFFLER, *Paris*, Leipzig 1908. — Marius BARROUX, *Le Département de la Seine et la Ville de Paris* (bibliography), Dumoulin, Paris 1910. — *Paris past and present*, special issue of *The Studio*, London 1915. — Louis HOURTICQ, *Paris*, Encyclopédie par l'image, Hachette, Paris 1924. — Marcel POÈTE, *Comment s'est formé Paris*, Hachette, Paris 1924. — Id., *Une vie de Cité : Paris de sa naissance à nos jours*, Picard, Paris 1925-1931, 3 vols. and one album. — *Paris, les anciens quartiers*, edited by Georges Cain, Paris n.d. (11 vols.). — Paul GINISTY, *Les anciens boulevards*, Hachette, Paris 1925. — Georges MONTORGUEIL, *Le vieux Montmartre*, Hachette, Paris 1925. — Pierre MAC-ORLAN, *Aux lumières de Paris*, Crès, Paris 1925. — Valery LARBAUD, *Rues et visages de Paris*, with 20 etchings by Charles Laborde, Paris 1926. — *Tableaux de Paris par divers écrivains*, Emile-Paul, Paris 1927. — Emile VERHAEREN, *Sensations*, Paris 1927. — Jean PRÉVOST, *Eiffel*, Rieder, Paris 1929. — Pierre MAC-ORLAN, *Images secrètes de Paris*, Paris 1930. — Lucien DUBECH and Pierre D'ESPEZEL, *Histoire de Paris*, Paris 1931, 2 vols. — Louis CHÉRONNET, *Paris vers 1900*, Chroniques du Jour, Paris 1932. — Héron DE VILLEFOSSE, *Paris vivant*, Paris 1932. — Id., *Singularités de Paris*, Grasset, Paris 1941. — John REWALD, *Paysages de Paris de Corot à Utrillo*, La Renaissance, Paris 1937. — Henri BIDOU, *Paris*, Gallimard, Paris 1938. — Paul VALÉRY, *Présence de Paris* (1940). — Jean AUBRY and Colette RAULT, *Paris, âges et visages* (poems), Paris 1943. — Jacques WILHELM, *Les peintres du paysage parisien, du XVe siècle à nos jours*, Paris 1944. — Louis CHÉRONNET, *Paris imprévu*, Paris 1946. — COLETTE, *Paris de ma fenêtre*, Paris 1948. — Léon-Paul FARGUE, *La flânerie à Paris*, Paris 1948. — *Huit siècles de vie britannique à Paris*, catalogue of the exhibition at the Musée Galliera, 1948. — Philippe LEFRANÇOIS, *Paris à travers les siècles*, photographs by René Jacque, Paris 1949. — Jean BABELON and J. JAQUIOT, *Histoire de Paris d'après les médailles, de la Renaissance au XXe siècle*, Paris 1951. — Jules BERTAUT, *Paris à travers les âges*, Hachette, Paris 1951. — *Les grands créateurs de Paris et leur œuvre*, catalogue of the exhibition at the Musée Carnavalet, Paris 1952. — Louis CHÉRONNET, *Paris tel qu'il fut*, Paris 1951. — *L'Esprit de Paris*, in *Plaisir de France*, 1951. — George POISSON, *La vie parisienne vue par les peintres*, F. Nathan, Paris 1953. — Marcel RAVAL, *Histoire de Paris*, Presses universitaires de France, Paris 1953. — *Paris im Bild seiner Maler*, catalogue of the Berlin exhibition, 1954. — Pierre COURTHION, *Montmartre*, Albert Skira, Geneva 1955.

INDEX OF NAMES

THE COLORPLATES

CONTENTS

THIS VOLUME, THE TWENTY-FIRST OF THE COLLECTION "THE
TASTE OF OUR TIME" WAS PRODUCED BY THE TECHNICAL STAFF
OF EDITIONS D'ART ALBERT SKIRA, FINISHED THE FIFTEENTH
DAY OF MARCH NINETEEN HUNDRED AND FIFTY-SEVEN.

TEXT AND ILLUSTRATIONS BY THE

COLOR STUDIO

AT IMPRIMERIES RÉUNIES S.A., LAUSANNE

PLATES ENGRAVED BY GUEZELLE ET RENOUARD, PARIS.

*Photographs by Louis Laniepce, Paris (pages 3, 9, 18, 28, 33, 34, 49, 58, 73, 77,
109, 110, 116, 120), by Zoltán Wegner, London (pages 27, 31, 86), by Hans Hinz,
Basel (pages 24, 38, 48, 52), by Henry B. Beville, Washington (pages 11, 17, 22,
23, 25, 30, 41, 42, 43, 44, 53, 54, 55, 59, 65, 67, 70, 74, 78, 80, 83, 85, 88, 89, 92,
97, 101, 107), by Photo Routhier, Paris (pages 15, 84, 90, 118), by Paul Bessem,
Amsterdam (pages 39, 45), by Harry Baskerville, Santa Barbara, Calif. (page 103)
and by courtesy of the photographic services of the Ny Carlsberg Glyptothek,
Copenhagen (page 63), the Hatfield Gallery, Santa Barbara, Calif. (page 66), the
Alfred Daber Gallery, Paris (page 69), and the National Gallery, Prague (page 93).*

PRINTED IN SWITZERLAND